The
CHANGEMAKER
A Leadership Story of
Courage and Character

Be the change!

By Tony Bridwell

Author of *The Maker* Series

"In today's age where people often don't listen and power seems to trump integrity, this is another wonderful fable that will stop and make you reflect on your choices and your approach to how you lead your life."

Kate Terrell
Human Resources Executive

"In the latest book in *The Maker* Series, Tony Bridwell once again introduces characters that are both relatable and inspiring in their leadership journey. *The Changemaker* reminds us that true leaders are those that demonstrate 'courageous generosity,' investing in others with their time, experience and connections."

Wendy Davidson
President, U.S. Specialty of Kellogg Company

"Another classic! Tony Bridwell's *The Maker* series has accelerated with *The Changemaker*! A captivating story about courage and character to continue shaping leadership today. Each chapter is filled with purposeful moments to guide us on our journey to be more influential through the power of authenticity, empathy, gratitude, and courage. Once you finish reading, you will be influenced to think about your own story and how you want it to be told in the days ahead. Get in the arena. This is a game changer!"

Bruce Waller, CRP, PHR, SHRM-CP
Vice President, Corporate Relocation,
Armstrong Relocation and Companies

"Tony has a talent of weaving thought-provoking lessons into enjoyable stories. In *The Changemaker*, you find yourself reflecting on your own leadership, character and influence. This book provides you with a balance of reflection and tactics. *The Changemaker* is a resource for your leadership toolbox you shouldn't be without."

Patti Niles
President/CEO,
Southwest Transplant Alliance

"*The Changemaker* challenged me to rethink my own approach to leadership. Tony weaves timeless concepts with modern day application–authentic influence–through a compelling story and characters. A great book to share with a leadership team!"

James Schmeltekopf
Executive Vice President, Wells Fargo Commercial Banking
(Central Region)

The

CHANGEMAKER

A Leadership Story
of Courage and Character

By Tony Bridwell

Author of *The Maker* Series

BB

This book is dedicated to
Mom and Dad,
I am forever grateful

FOREWORD

Tony Bridwell's *The Maker* series has been a valuable part of my leadership journey. This latest installment is no exception. I was first introduced to the power of leadership storytelling from Tony at a pivotal point in my own personal journey.

Several years ago, I had the opportunity to partner with Tony as I was leading the integration of a newly formed 34,000-employee, global organization, navigating deep cultural and business challenges. His powerful storytelling, contagious energy, and personal investment in those around him made a lasting impact on our whole team. As he and I worked with the team to define our desired future, Tony helped me build skills of leadership visioning. He also gave me a copy of *The Kingmaker*. I promptly read it in one sitting!

In both his work and his writing, Tony is continuously helping others fulfill their respective purposes. This newest installment, *The Changemaker*, had a profoundly inspirational impact on me.

For those readers who have explored all of *The Maker* books, this will enable you to reacquaint yourself with some of your favorite characters. Follow them as they transition through major life decisions, guided by their personal "board of directors." For those who are new to Tony's stories, you will be transported to New York, Dallas, and other recent battlefields to join a small group of colleagues and lifelong friends as they support themselves and each other. The story is told through the eyes of Sara, the Chief of Staff for a US Representative. Unexpectedly, she finds herself without her trusted mentor and searching for her true purpose.

Sara and those around her must learn to bring character and courage to life's challenges. We see that there are times to lean into a challenging engagement, perhaps getting bruised a bit. There are also times when it is right to walk away, again with integrity and courage.

Many personal journeys require rebirth along the way, mine included. This rebirth is often what is needed to find our true purposes, requiring courage to leap into the unknown, while depending on trusted guides to see us through. *The Changemaker* brings to life the power of reimagined futures and the joy of making them a reality. Every character has a gift to share with both their loved ones and the reader.

No matter where you are on your personal leadership journey, there is something to learn from *The Changemaker* characters. Leading with authenticity is one of the most powerful qualities one can bring to a team. Tony's book addresses the impact of authentic influence–being your true self and helping others do the same. The conclusion: your ability to change the world around you comes from your ability to influence others. Authentic influence is the key.

Our protagonist, Sara, learns that we all deserve a chance for rebirth, a second opportunity to find and fulfill our life's purposes. To steal a line from the book, "It is in the messiness of the arena that you find your purpose." After experiencing these characters and their journeys, you will welcome the ability to step into your own arena and you will learn to embrace the messiness that is your unique journey. If you walk away from this story with one key call to action it is that your arena awaits.

—LORRAINE MARTIN

INTRODUCTION

A friend used a phrase over dinner recently that captured my attention: "Our microwave society has zapped the true flavor out of life." He further explained that our "need it now" culture costs us the spice of life. Would it surprise you to learn this person is a self-proclaimed foodie? While I'm not looking to debate the merits of the microwave, I do understand his metaphor-*when we move through life at hyper-speed, we cannot taste the joy of the journey.*

This fourth installment in *The Maker* Series is all about embracing a sudden shift in life's direction. In *The Changemaker*, Sara Davis, Chief of Staff for powerful Congresswoman Clara Becker, has arrived at a crossroads in her life. With Congresswoman Becker unavailable to guide her, Sara must choose her next steps. A surprise discovery of Clara's video diary gives Sara the courage to rethink her course and realize that she has the power of transformative character. Sara's journey, and the wisdom she uncovers along the way, is a story that unveils this truth for everyone. Filled with Key Insights and meaningful Mentoring Moments, the reader will discover nuggets in the narrative meant to strengthen character, expand influence, and embolden courage. Ultimately, Sara discovers that the joy *is* in the journey.

Practical parables are my preferred style as I seek to speak into this truth. While the persuasive "how to" book has become the standard genre for many readers, I offer a different approach. A fable restores a sense of discovery and adds vivid flavor to the mental taste buds that have been zapped by self-help lists. With today's reader in mind, the length of the story is about two and a half to three hours of reading time. That equates to three workouts, or a flight from Dallas to New York, or if you listen to Audible-three commutes to work. In other words, longer than a microwave meal, but still shorter than Thanksgiving dinner. The goal is to tell a story in a reasonable amount of time while nourishing the mind in the process.

Frequently I am asked if a reader must read the other books in the series first. Each story is written to stand alone; however, characters in *The Kingmaker* and *The Newsmaker* show up in each story, creating a connection between each installment. The focus of each story is slightly different with some thoughtful overlap. In *The Changemaker*, it was important to unpack the idea of character and gently expose new vulnerabilities in the story. For those who have read the other books in the series, this will provide greater insight into the continued journey of each character.

I am deeply humbled by each person who invests in these stories. You are greatly appreciated. My hope and prayer for those willing to listen is that it is never too late for *you* to become a changemaker–and change the world.

The
DARK DAY

Sara's pace increased as she walked south on 5th Avenue, navigating through the early holiday crowds. The city was unusually busy as shoppers and tourists intermingled with the local city dwellers in search of the latest discount. The crisp fall air prompted Sara to pull the collar of her jacket up around her ears, providing warmth and a small buffer of protection from the people around her. On most days, Sara fastidiously learned the names of everyone she encountered, making each one feel like the most important person in the room by the time she left. Today, Sara found herself envious of the throng of people passing her on the crowded street, their headphones protecting them from the surrounding mass of humanity.

As the Chief of Staff for a United States Representative, Sara was no stranger to large crowds of people. After earning a degree in journalism from the University of Texas, she had completed law school at Southern Methodist University and jumped right into the crowded race towards a Washington D.C. career. Sara had lost her father at a young age. Sara's mom, Anne, had worked as an attorney to support Sara's education while instilling in Sara the confidence to become a strong, self-assured woman. Sara quickly realized that communication came easy for her and the opportunities were many. Choosing to intern with a Federal judge in Dallas was the door that opened Sara to the one person who would set her apart from the crowd and forever change her life.

Arriving at the stoplight on the corner of 46th Street, Sara stood silently amongst a growing volume of pedestrians, consumed in thought. Looking up, she observed the grandeur of the towering bookstore across the street. Sara's heart beat faster as a flood of memories overcame her thoughts. The light turned green and she was swept forward with the crowd, involuntarily moving closer to her destination.

Streams of people filed into the bookstore, most of them focused on meeting the star attraction, *New York Times* best-selling author, Carson Stewart. Sara paused at the entrance, captivated by the standing sign that featured Carson's picture. His life-sized caricature directed patrons to the back of the store where he was conducting the book signing.

It had been only two years since Sara first met Carson and joined him on his tumultuous journey. Carson's fall from grace back then was nothing short of spectacular. As a rising superstar in the world of syndicated media, Carson was at the top of his game as a weekly columnist for the Nation's largest newspaper. That is, until his drinking overwhelmed him, driving him to make the one unforgivable mistake in the media business: a plagiarized article.

Carson's tough, some would say cynical, approach to life caused many to jump on the "take down Carson" bandwagon, which fueled his fall. The final blow was a result of Carson's consumption of the liquid vice which sealed his plummet from fame. All but a few real friends, those who were willing to get close to the most toxic person in media, rallied behind Carson to pull him out of the ashes. The pivotal moment presented itself when Brian Palmer offered Carson a second chance on an article about the integrous Congresswoman, Clara Becker. Some, including Carson, would say this offer was wholly undeserved. But Brian saw something in Carson that others refused to acknowledge–especially those who enjoyed knocking Carson out of the game.

Between Brian and a close friend Joe, they picked up the broken pieces of Carson Stewart and glued together the parts of his soul that restored his true purpose. Since that moment, Sara had heard Carson say on more than one occasion, "Sometimes your purpose finds you." Little did Carson know that the path Brian paved for him would not only lead to a more epic fall-by means of a failed suicide attempt, a scandal within the Beltway, and failed assassination-but it would also bring Carson face-to-face with two people who would radically change his life for good.

Frozen, Sara stood a few yards from the entrance, working up the courage to step into the flow of people entering the store. It had been two months since Sara had seen Carson. The last time they had been in the same space together was referred to as *The Dark Day* by the media–and dark it was. The mix of emotions rushing over her created a light-headed sensation and an unnatural wave of anxiety. Spinning around, Sara took several deliberate steps away from the store's entrance.

"Maybe a cup of coffee at Bryant Park will calm my nerves," she said loudly enough to prompt one person to respond, "They have coffee in the store." Not realizing what was happening Sara looked up to make eye contact with the person making the casual comment. The return look of compassion from the total stranger, even for New York standards, took Sara by surprise. It was in that moment, seeing the expression on the stranger's face, that Sara realized tears were streaming uncontrollably down her cheeks.

The memories of the dark day two months ago prompted an instant flood of emotions. That was the day they laid her mentor and friend, Clara Becker, to rest following a sudden and shocking heart attack. The state funeral for Clara was attended by dignitaries, colleagues and friends-appropriately fitting for such a monumental figure in public life. Lying in state inside the United States Capitol building, the sitting President provided a portion of the eulogy before she was flown back to her home state of Texas for a final private ceremony. Sara was numb through the whole thing, carefully making arrangements to commemorate a life well-lived.

No one saw the events of the dark day approaching. At one moment, Clara and Sara were discussing plans for a book signing tour when suddenly, Clara paused, gazed at Sara with a knowing look and whispered, "I love you," before closing her eyes and slumping over in her chair. Paralyzed in the moment and incapable of determining what was reality or possibly a dream, Sara finally exhaled and caught her breath. Utilizing the full force of her lungs she screamed, "Call 911!"

Within moments, the Capitol Police were onsite performing CPR. The Congresswoman's staff stood in disbelief as numerous first responders rushed in to assist. Multiple EMT's worked over Clara as they strapped her to a gurney and rushed her to George Washington University Hospital. There, the

Head of Emergency Medicine had the gut-wrenching job of calling the time of death for the Congresswoman of the Great State of Texas, Clara Becker.

Wiping the tears from her face, Sara dabbed her eyes gently, trying to avoid a mascara meltdown. Taking a deep breath, Sara turned toward the revolving door. Timing her entry perfectly, Sara stepped inside the rapidly moving portal and paused, immobile in the main hall of the massive bookstore. Her eyes deliberately scanned the horizon searching for a mass of people gathered at her reluctant destination.

Fixated on the spot, Sara began moving slowing towards the crowd. A line gently wrapped around the store as eager people stood patiently holding their copy of *The Lawmaker*, anxiously waiting for the author to place his name on the inside cover. As she walked past several in line, Sara's eyes were drawn to a young lady reading the back cover of the book. There Sara saw the picture of Carson. Her steps slowed as she took in the moment, realizing the headshot was from a joint sitting where Carson and Sara had taken pictures together. Carson had told Sara it was a photoshoot for the book but wanted her to join him in a few shots. Secretly, Sara had hoped Carson had planned the day as a surprise and that the pictures would be used for an announcement of sorts.

Sara quickly refocused her thoughts to the journey at hand, finding both the end of the line and the author. From a vantage point just short of the signing table, Sara paused to mentally map out her approach. Abigail, Carson's publisher rep, was feeding the next person's book to Carson in order to create a steady flow of signatures. The process only slowed for the occasional photo and handshake.

Moving into Abigail's blind spot, Sara positioned herself behind Carson. Sara was within a few feet of Carson when Abigail finally noticed her. Making eye contact, Abigail smiled warmly, silently communicating her sincere joy at Sara's presence. Even that brief glimpse acknowledging Sara broke the pace of the line. Carson looked up at Abigail, curious what had caused her shift of focus.

"Everything okay?"

Abigail smiled, still holding the next customer's book in her hand, and gently nodded toward Sara. Carson's eyes grew wide as he slowly turned and recognized the one woman who he loved more deeply than anyone in his life.

Slowly Carson rose from the old wooden chair and enfolded Sara in a warm, lingering embrace. Disregarding the hundred or more cell phone cameras rolling video and snapping rapid-fire pictures of the tender moment, Carson resolutely tightened his embrace as Sara gradually melted into his arms. Eventually, Carson placed his strong hands on Sara's shoulders, moving just far enough apart for him to gaze into her deep blue eyes. Leaning close to her ear, Carson softly whispered, "I've missed you more than you can imagine."

Sara could sense the moisture building in her eyes once again as she leaned into the strong chest of the man she loved. "I'm here now."

The
MESSAGE

The next hour flew by until they closed out the final customer and photo op with Carson. Abigail was putting away the last of the materials when Sara came alongside her, reaching out to offer a generous embrace.

"Thank you for helping Carson through the last few months. I'm not sure what he would have done without you," Sara said in a tone of genuine sincerity.

Abigail smiled and gave Sarah a squeeze. "It was my pleasure to serve. He has been doing better over the last few days but the stress of the media tour may be too much for him." Abigail pulled back and added, "Your presence will do miracles for his spirits."

Sara's eyes brightened at hearing the encouraging words from Abigail. "What can I do to help out here?" Sara's voice was particularly upbeat, as if trying to choke back another rush of tears.

Abigail squeezed Sara's hands tightly. "I'm almost finished here. You go be with Carson." As Abigail placed the last piece of promotional material into the plastic container, she offered one last thought, "But I would love to steal you away for a drink if you are in the City for a few days. Just let me know when you are available."

"I will see how Carson is doing and text you," Sara offered. "It will be lovely to catch up."

"Perfect." Abigail placed the plastic container on the rolling dolly for her assistant to take back to the office. "I will look forward to your text."

Carson wiggled his fingers until he could feel the blood rushing back to the numb fingertips of his signing hand. After signing nearly 500 copies, he was beginning to wonder if his hand would curl into an arthritic knot and refuse to release. The bookstore manager unknowingly made matters worse with an overly enthusiastic congratulatory handshake, grateful for a successful signing event.

Sara, back on her game, recognized the manager's enthusiasm and gently interceded as she had done thousands of times for Clara. "May I steal the famous author away for a quick photo?" she said with the disarming smile she had perfected over of the years. With one unbroken move, she whisked Carson away from the center of attention to a quiet corner of the store. Once safe from the public eye, Carson leaned close to Sara and gently graced her lips with a soft kiss. The peaceful moment was short-lived as a wandering customer stumbled upon them among the books.

Ushering Sara outside, Carson effortlessly waved down a cab and automatically set the course for *Joe's Place*.

"As much as I want to see Joe, is there any chance we could hide out at your place, order dinner in and just reconnect?" Sara asked, resting her head on Carson's shoulder.

"New stop." Carson directed the cabbie to the address of his Village apartment.

Sara didn't fully acknowledge her level of anxiety until she allowed herself to relax against Carson's chest. The trip from mid-town to the Village passed by quickly. Sliding out of the cab, Sara was overcome by a rush of new emotions while standing in front of Carson's apartment. Climbing the steps together, Carson opened the door to allow Sara to enter first. Once inside, Carson located the number for Joe's Pizza while reviewing the slim contents of his refrigerator.

"One large everything and a couple of Cokes," Carson said with a subtle hint of a New Yorker accent. "Dinner is on the way," he proclaimed to Sara who had found her way to the one new piece of furniture in the apartment: the sofa.

Carson sat across from Sara so he could absorb all her beauty. Sara smiled softly, warmed by the glow of his admiration.

"High/low?" She uttered a subtle phrase the two of them coined after they started dating. This query forced the other to be present in the conversation, eliminating the standard responses of *fine* and *good*. Carson didn't hesitate.

"My high is having you here after witnessing 500 people waiting for me to sign copies of my book. My high is humbling for sure on both accounts."

"And your low?" Sara continued, ensuring Carson wouldn't change the subject.

"The pit in my stomach from missing Clara," Carson responded, his voice trailing off with a sigh.

"I miss her, too, Carson," Sara offered empathically, just as the bell rang to announce that dinner had arrived.

The night began to feel a more familiar shade of normal as Carson and Sara worked their way through their favorite New York pizza.

"Be careful not to get crumbs on my new sofa," Carson chided with the recognizable lively tone in his voice. Sara smiled as she folded over her pizza and took a bite. A never-ending string of mozzarella cheese suspended gently between Sara's lips, and the folded slice of pizza now extended nearly an arm's length away from Sara's mouth. She smiled as her eyes widened and crossed, letting out a slight giggle and allowing herself a moment of delight. Carson reached up to rescue Sara from the hot and steamy cheese creature refusing to release its prey. With great care, Carson removed the only barrier between him and Sara's soft lips. Leaning in, he gently pressed his lips to those of Sara, causing her to consciously catch her breath. With pizza still suspended in mid-air, Sara tilted her head and closed her eyes, surrendering her body to the warm tingling sensation that began in the pit of her stomach and completely engulfed her entire body.

Carson's fingers moved slowly through Sara's hair as his strong hand cradled her head. With much care, he released his lips from hers, hovering in place for a moment. Sara could feel Carson's heart beat quicker, which produced a reflex within Sara to pull Carson closer until they could simultaneously feel the rise and fall of each other's chests.

Sara, still present in her lover's embrace, finally opened her eyes to see Carson and, in that moment, she knew he was going to be okay. Now, if she could just sort out her own emotions, life could once again move forward with purpose.

****

Abigail tapped out the text message to Sara. "Lunch tomorrow?" Sara answered immediately, "Would love to. When and where?" "Fig and Olive on 52nd, 12:30?" Abigail typed back. "Perfect, looking forward to catching up."

The bright Mediterranean design immediately invigorated the senses upon entering the restaurant. Sara was running a few minutes behind, so she informed the hostess her friend was waiting in the upstairs area. With an affirming nod, the young hostess escorted Sara up the staircase to reveal a separate seating area, effectively doubling the size of the restaurant.

Scanning the full dining room, Sara spotted Abigail at a table close to the front windows. After a brief hug, the two settled into the comfortable wicker chairs overlooking 52nd street below. Abigail was perfectly City casual today in jeans and a black cashmere turtleneck sweater, her long black hair pulled tightly into a flawless ponytail. Her soft caramel skin accented her ruby red lipstick. Abigail's parents were born in India, but she was raised in London. Abigail remained there until she seized an opportunity to study at Princeton during her first semester at University in the UK. One semester was all it took for her to decide to stay in the U.S. Now, as a naturalized citizen, Abigail considered the City as much her home as London. If not for her impeccable English accent, most never recognized she wasn't from the City.

New York City was ceaselessly busy and today was no different. Sara, after all these years, was still amazed at the sheer volume of people moving throughout the city.

"Do you ever get tired of all the people?" Sara started the conversation.

"I've never really thought about it. Having been raised in the heart of London, it feels normal to endure the crowds," Abigail replied, adding slowly, "Admittedly, the holidays do seem a bit more crowded than in recent years."

"Thank you for inviting me to lunch," Sara offered as she placed the menu off to one side, having pre-selected what she would order. Old habits were hard to break and previewing a menu ahead of time was just one practice Clara taught Sara when meeting over lunch. Clara would say, "Knowing what you want before you go demonstrates confidence in the first moments of any meeting."

Abigail noticed Sara's subtle move and asked, "Have you been here before?"

"No, but the Fig and Olive Salad comes highly recommended," Sara offered almost out of reflex. Abigail's smile indicated a deepening approval of the strong woman sitting across from her.

"I haven't had that yet so we will make that two," Abigail offered just as their waiter appeared to take their order.

Once the waiter removed the last dish from the table, Abigail reached into her handbag to reveal a white USB stick with the letters CB/SD handwritten on the side. Placing it gently on the table, the writing was visible to Sara, and Abigail let Sara's eyes connect with the writing before she spoke.

"Midway through Carson's interviews with Clara, she realized how much she enjoyed the process for writing the book. There were so many thoughts coming out of her extraordinary mind, she didn't want to stop," Abigail began.

Sara sat upright and immobile as she carefully listened to what Abigail was explaining. "One day Clara asked if I would stay a bit longer to add a few more details to the interview. She wanted me to show her how to create a separate file for additional recordings," Abigail added while maintaining eye contact with Sara. "When the interview portion of the writing process was complete, Clara brought me this USB drive and asked that I give it to you when we finished the book tour." Abigail's words trailed off slightly as she fought back the emotion of reliving the conversation with Clara. "My instructions were to tell you the password would be obvious given where you come from," Abigail said with a hint of curiosity as the words exited her mouth.

Sara wanted to reach for the small memory stick but couldn't convince her brain to move her arms. Quietly she rested in the moment, replaying each word from Abigail over in her mind. The password riddle was easy: "thegreatstateoftexas." It was the obvious answer as she and the Congresswoman had used it many times. The larger, more intriguing riddle, was what content would she find on the drive?

The moment was interrupted as the waiter appeared, almost on cue, to ask if either of them would like a coffee. Simultaneously, they responded, "Yes!" producing a well-timed grin of relief. Sara, seizing the moment, carefully reached across the table to retrieve the precious treasure.

"Thank you," was all Sara could muster at the moment. Abigail nodded as she reached to touch Sara's hand, her gentle squeeze signaling assurance all would be okay. It was in that instant that Sara confirmed she had a new trusted friend in Abigail.

Sara needed time and a private place to open the drive from Clara. After hugging Abigail and thanking her for an unforgettable lunch, Sara hopped into the back of the City cab. "Joe's

Place, 7th and Christopher in the Village," Sara directed in a noticeably excited tone. Retrieving her phone from her bag, Sara texted her uncle Joe, although she still referred to him as just *Joe*.

> Heading your way. Busy?" she texted. There was barely a delay in the response.
> "Always here-and never too busy for you," Joe replied.

The text brought a quick smile to Sara's face as she stared out the window of the cab. She felt the small drive pressed firmly in her hand, locked safely as if she were guarding national secrets. More than once in her career had Sara been in possession of vital information. Top Secret Clearance was required for her role as Clara Becker's Chief of Communications. Nothing she had been exposed to in the past, however, could match the gravity of the information she was holding in her hand at that moment. Little did Sara know it was even greater than she realized.

Arriving at the front of Joe's Place produced a new wave of emotions. It was only two years prior that Sara discovered Joseph Hamilton-or Joe as everyone called him-was her uncle. In a twist of events straight out of a spy novel, Sara learned her uncle had also known Clara from his youth. Evidently, their serious romance came to a regrettable end when Joe disappeared into the dark ops of the military. Back then, his love for Clara could not match his fear of widowing her as a result of his highly specialized branch of operations. A master of tactical skill, the military offered him refuge from the one area in life he lacked expertise-his ability to express his feelings towards the one he loved. His unexpected reunion with Clara two years ago had rekindled that love–only to retreat once more upon the news of her untimely death.

Upon entering the bar, Sara's senses shifted into overdrive. Even though it had been months since her last visit, each smell, sound, and sight flooded her mind with the comfort of familiarity. Sara could feel her breathing becoming deeper and more deliberate as she paused for a brief moment just inside the old front door. Her eyes scanned the busy lunch crowd, seeking out Joe's comforting smile. Behind the bar was the newest member of the Joe's team, Marisa, whom he discovered working in the Meat Packing District and persuaded to join him. Rumor was that they may be dating–providing a slow thaw in the heart of a man whose love had been frozen too many times.

"He's in the back," a voice rose over the room of noisy patrons. Looking in the direction of the voice, Sara made eye contact with Marisa. Signaling back with a semi-sure wave of acknowledgement, Sara made her way to the back of the bar. Descending the stairs, Sara hugged the wall as the lone waitstaff hustled up one side of the old wooden stairs carrying a burger and fries from the kitchen below. Expanding the kitchen was Marisa's idea and based on the burger sales-the sole offering on the lunch menu-it was a good bet.

Entering the kitchen, Sara was taken aback by the efficiency of the operation. With the addition of only two other people, Joe was able to produce hundreds of burgers per day. Arthur Martinez, a retired Vietnam War vet, was handling the bulk of the load while Joe provided the final details for each basket of burger magic. The third employee, Bethany Patterson, or Patterson as she was better known, was a veteran of the Gulf War. She was dropping fresh cut fries and keeping the dishware clean, a position Joe hired from the 3rd Street Shelter's Project Renewal effort.

When Joe first visited the Shelter, he immediately recognized an untapped potential in Patterson, which stemmed from her storied, military experience. At the time, she was homeless and staying only temporarily at the shelter. Joe understood firsthand how difficult it was to transition away from the structure and support of a military team who placed their lives into each other's hands every day. He had witnessed many veterans struggle to reintegrate into an unstructured society that was sometimes ignorant or unappreciative of military service. Serving down range changes everything. Patterson was now different. Few people in the world could fully identify with Patterson's experiences and the depth of her wounds.

Joe recalled lightly brushing the three tightly grouped scars on his chest upon meeting Patterson. The corresponding marks on his back were evidence of his deeply personal understanding of the daily torment she battled. He instinctively hired her on the spot. Joe was determined to make sure Patterson's own scar tissue didn't restrict the healing of her own wounded heart.

"Quite the change from the sleepy little dive I first walked into a few years ago," Sara said with admiration.

Without turning around, Joe responded, "Not a dive, only a dump with aspirations of becoming a dive someday. If Marisa had it her way, we would be the next *Shake Shack*."

Sara smiled. "What I can do to help?" She took off her jacket and placed it on the lone chair in the room. In that moment, she realized the zip drive was still locked in her hand as she froze to look at her clinched fist.

Turning towards her with three baskets of burgers, Joe began, "We have it…" He stopped before he could finish the sentence as he caught his first glance of his niece, paused in the moment, staring intently at the exposed drive in her palm. From her expression, he knew Sara was holding something of great importance. "Patterson, run this upstairs for me." Joe's tone was subdued as he held out the food.

"Roger that." Patterson grabbed the baskets in full stride and headed for the stairs.

Sara's body began to melt as a single tear rolled down her cheek. Taking off his apron, Joe never broke eye contact with Sara as he said, "Arthur, you got this?"

"Piece of cake, boss. Rush is over," Arthur replied as he began to scrape the flattop grill.

Picking up Sara's coat in one hand, he wrapped his other arm around her and pulled her close. Joe could feel Sara gently sob as she buried her head deep into Joe's chest. "We need some fresh air. Don't want you smelling like a burger joint," Joe said in a tender voice. He could feel her smile through her tears.

"I would be proud to smell like a burger joint if it meant spending time with you."

Placing her coat on her shoulders, Joe motioned upstairs. At the top of the stairs was a door leading out into the back ally. Joe texted Marisa as they were climbing the narrow stairway.

"Heading out for a bit with Sara," Joe typed.
"No worries, all good here," Marisa quickly responded.

Once they were outside, Joe directed Sara toward a narrow passage leading to a hidden garden beneath the tower buildings surrounding Joe's Place. Weaving their way through the garden, they emerged on 10th Street, angling right towards the bookstore beneath Joe's apartment. The stroll allowed Sara to collect her thoughts as Joe walked silently next to her. He could sense something was going on in her head and quickly drew the conclusion that it somehow involved Clara. Upon arriving at the bookstore, Joe slipped around the corner to the obscure black door located in a discrete corner of the historic building. Unlocking the 100-year-old door, Joe and Sara walked in and began the trek up the two flights of stairs to Joe's studio on the third level.

Entering the apartment, Sara's intuition confirmed the fact that Joe was indeed dating Marisa. She began to smile.

"How long have you and Marisa been serious?"

Joe stopped mid-motion as he reached for a two cold bottles of water. "What makes you think we are dating?"

"Come on, Uncle Joe, you aren't the only one with super spy powers," she said with a slight smirk. Her smile softened. "I'm just happy you have found companionship these days." She left the rest unspoken, the silence betraying the lingering emotions they shared over the loss of Clara.

Retrieving the water, Joe turned and cleared his throat—and the years of unspoken emotion that threatened to exit his lips. "We didn't take a walk to talk about me. We should perhaps talk about that zip drive you have had a death grip on since you walked into the bar," he successfully deflected to the issue at hand. Sara loosened the emerald-colored cashmere scarf from around her neck. Slipping into the worn leather reading chair, Joe's favorite spot for a book and coffee, Sara exhaled a day's worth of anxiety. Slowly raising her hand, she exposed the zip drive for Joe to view. "It's from Clara," Sara said in a soft whisper.

Joe carefully placed the bottle of water on the 1930's side table next to Sara. As Sara reached for the water, she noticed an old book on the table. Sara's hand froze midair as her mind processed where she had seen this book before. Her memory quickly recalled seeing this first edition, Ernest Hemingway's *For Whom the Bell Tolls*, in Clara's office amongst the cherished items on her credenza. Gently reaching for the book, she picked it up, running her hand over the tattered cover. Slowly, she opened to the first page, revealing the multiple inscriptions between Joe and Clara.

The chair Sara was sitting in was positioned perfectly within the apartment to take advantage of the daylight streaming through the curtainless windows. The sun cast a perfect glow upon the writing, "*To my guardian angel, I am eternally grateful. Clara.*"

Sara smiled as her eyes lingered on the intimate inscription. For a brief moment, Sara had forgotten about the drive in her grip. Holding out his hand, Joe softly responded, "May I?" Sara closed the cover of the old book and placed the drive in Joe's hand feeling the weight of a thousand questions exit her body.

Producing a laptop from the messenger bag next to his chair, Joe plugged the drive in to discover a password entry box. Anticipating the question, Sara offered, "*The great state of Texas*, all one word." She then grinned at Joe for added effect. Tapping on the keys, Joe entered the password to reveal a series of file folders with various names and dates. Double clicking on what appeared to be the earliest date, Joe discovered a video file. A couple of clicks expanded the video to full screen and revealed an image of Clara. He carefully pressed the play arrow.

"Hi, Sara," Clara began. "Carson showed me how to use the camera during our interview sessions. He is much more talented than I ever gave him credit for," she continued with a grin. "All this self-talk for the book started me thinking. There is so much more I want to share with you, so while it is fresh in my head, I am going to record a few extra videos just for you. The book has a considerable amount of information, but there are insights I've been holding back that are only meant for you. The more Carson tugs the past out of me through his interviews, the more clearly I realize how much I appreciate having you in my life. I see a great deal of myself in you. Only the best parts, of course," Clara qualified with her classic laugh.

Hearing the voice of her friend and mentor, as though they were sharing tea together in the same room, prompted the tears to stream ceaselessly down Sara's face. Clara's recording continued.

"I am learning a great deal about myself by going through this process with Carson. In today's interview, something dawned on me that I wanted to share with you. He was asking me about the 'key to success' in my life. The key to what many refer to as 'my success' is based on what I call 'courageous generosity.' I'm now realizing the enormous courage required in order to be generous with our resources, and most importantly, our time. But even greater, Sara, I realized that real courage is required when we are generous with how we connect with others. Many take this for granted, but understand that the true key to enduring success is courageous generosity with our time and connections."

Sara had allowed her body to fully relax in the leather chair as Clara's message warmly engulfed her. She fought the desire to ask questions of the video as if it were some kind of artificial intelligence avatar. And yet, somehow, Clara was still able to read and respond to the question in Sara's mind.

"I know what you are thinking, Sara," Clara announced with a sly grin. "Why is generosity with our time and connections not enough; why does it require courage? Well, for most people, generosity is something that happens at a surface level. We give of our time when it is convenient. Same goes for our connections. People tend to be generous with their connections to others when they benefit from the connection. Sara, I've learned that our ability to truly make a difference only stems from the connections we make that require courage," Clara declared in a tone very familiar to Sara, a tone she recognized from many conversations over the years. "You are also wondering how to better define courage. For that, I would direct you to ask your Uncle Joe." She concluded this final statement with a wink.

Joe paused in his own discomfort and added, "Do you want to watch another one or call it a day?"

Sara hesitated for a moment and, without speaking, just gently shook her head to indicate no. "Copy the drive onto your laptop if you have room," she said after a few seconds had passed.

"Are you sure? These seem fairly personal," Joe responded.

"Well, if by *personal*, you are pointing to *both of us*, then yes they are. Based on the first one it looks like you are getting dragged into this conversation if you like it or not," Sara said with more perk in her voice than she had had in the last several days.

"Any idea what she was referring to when she said to ask you about courage?" Sara asked while sipping her water to relieve the dryness dominating her mouth.

Joe slowly closed the laptop, reclining in the old ladderback chair and causing it to creak under his cumbersome posture. From behind his thick beard, a grin appeared. "Before I shipped out for duty, Clara and I had a conversation about courage. I remember it because she was the one who came to my rescue that day." He paused and reflected on that memory.

"Clara was like that," Sara added. Joe's smile widened.

"That is what made her who she was."

"So how did she come to your rescue?" Sara asked in a tone indicating she wasn't going to stop asking until he fully explained.

"Clara had an ability to read people. She could sense I was second guessing my decision. Deep inside, admittedly, I was afraid. On the outside I would never show it or let anyone else know. But, Clara knew. She told me courage was not the lack of fear, but our willingness to face our fear with vulnerability-to get into the arena and dare greatly," Joe said with passion in his voice.

Sara's expression registered some impatience, and Joe realized she hungered for more detail.

"I've never told anyone, but it was Clara who inspired me to read. My thirst for knowledge was ignited the moment she shared her heart on what it meant to be courageous." Joe stood up from his chair and made his way to the full wall of floor-to-ceiling book cases. At first glance, most would consider his apartment as overflow storage for the bookstore below. Hundreds of volumes of books from all genres lined the wall of the historic space. With great precision he pulled a book from the shelf, opening it to a well-read dogeared page.

"Clara told me she was quoting one of her favorite Presidents, Teddy Roosevelt. In one of his more famous speeches, entitled *Citizenship in a Republic*, he said these words." Holding the book up like a holy document, Joe carefully placed his finger at the appropriate place on the page, a page which had multiple lines and notes in the margins. He began to read in his deep, authoritative voice as if channeling the late great president, *"It is not the critic who counts; not the man who points out how the strong man stumbles, or where the doer of deeds could have done them better. The credit belongs to the man who is actually in the arena, whose face is marred by dust and sweat and blood; who strives valiantly; who errs, who comes short again and again, because there is no effort without error and shortcoming; but who does actually strive to do the deeds; who knows great enthusiasms, the great devotions; who spends himself in a worthy cause; who at the best knows in the end the triumph of high achievement, and who at the worst, if he fails, at least fails while daring greatly, so that his place shall never be with those cold and timid souls who neither know victory nor defeat."*

Sara noticed a slight hesitation in Joe's voice as he read aloud, a delicate pause as he read the final few lines revealing the flash flood of memories from years past. Closing the book with great care, Joe held it gently in his strong hands. Instead of replacing the book in its well-worn space on the shelf, Joe tucked it under his arm, deciding to hang on to this one for the time being.

Sara stood quietly at the door as she waited for her car to arrive. Noting the book firmly enveloped in Joe's arms, she glanced again at the old Hemingway book lying on the side table. "You know, sometimes it is okay to put a book back on the shelf. It doesn't mean it is forgotten. You can pull it out anytime and honor the one who gave it to you," she said softly. Sara kissed Joe on the cheek and slipped out the door to her waiting car.

As she departed, Joe turned and stared at the Hemingway novel on the side table. Carefully, he picked it up and slid into the spot left vacant by *Citizens of the Republic*.

"You were always the real guardian angel," he whispered, his fingers lingering on the spine of the book as he blinked back a lifetime of tears. He turned to watch Sara climb into the car through the frosted window.

"And I know you are watching over her."

The
DINNER

Street side, Sara climbed into the backseat of the Toyota Prius and smiled for the duration of the ride, realizing this was a perfect metaphor for Joe. Sara felt the vibration of her phone for the first time in hours. While focused on deciphering the zip drive, she had blocked out all surrounding distractions until she was able to view the mysterious message from Clara. Retrieving her phone from her coat pocket, she discovered she had a number of text messages and a missed call from Carson. Her phone also displayed the time, making Sara acutely aware of the hour of day.

Carson and Sara had dinner plans with Kyle and Emily Ellis tonight. Kyle was CEO of Ellis International and longtime friend of Clara. Kyle's firm was an international powerhouse PR agency. To a select few people, Kyle's reputation was renowned as the *kingmaker*-guiding and crafting the careers of seemingly ordinary people while transforming their greatest potential into the true powerbrokers of the world.

"Not ignoring you. Was catching up with Joe and lost track of time."

Carson's message appeared on the screen, "Tell Joe I said hi. He may be wondering if I'm still in the City since I haven't been to his place in a month."

"I'm heading to my hotel to change. Would it be easier to meet at the restaurant?"

"See you there. Love you."

Sara paused as she read his last two words. She felt a warmth rush over her as her fingers gently touched her lips. She smiled with consideration and quickly replied, "Love you, too."

Once in her room, Sara began the process of the quick change, a procedure she had perfected during years of working with Clara. After showering and wrapping herself in a warm bathrobe, Sara stole an uncharacteristic moment to sit on the end of her bed and take in the spectacular views of the park. Her mind drifted back to the first time she had dined with Carson in the City. She remembered agonizing over her attire that night. Tonight would be a less stressful selection. She chose a simple, deep navy blue dress, an impeccable winter white coat, and over-the-knee boots.

Quality Italian was an eight-minute walk for Sara, and she was grateful for her warm, sturdy boots. While waiting at the light at 5th Avenue, Sara typed a text to Carson.

"Heading that way. Should be there in a few minutes."

"Perfect timing. I'll wait for you at the front door," he promptly typed back.

The crowded corner moved forward in unison once the light changed. Sara timed her steps perfectly to maintain her position within the mass of people crossing the street. At the corner of 6th Avenue, Sara angled to the north side of 57th and covered the last few steps to the bright red doors of the restaurant. Carson had spotted Sara's white coat, and he quickened his steps to greet her just before she made it to the entrance.

Placing both hands on her shoulders, he gently pulled her close for a kiss. Sara fully embraced Carson as if she hadn't seen him in weeks, even though they had been together earlier that day.

"You look amazing," Carson whispered.

"Thank you," Sara replied with a shy smile.

At that moment, a black Mercedes pulled along the curb. The back door swung open and Kyle and Emily stepped out of the backseat.

"Perfect timing you two," Carson said, spotting Kyle first.

"Great to see you, Carson." Kyle slapped Carson's back in a friendly greeting. Sara had shuffled around them to greet Emily who was making her way around the car from the opposite side.

"Hello, Emily," Sara smiled. Emily enfolded Sara in a warm hug.

"So great to see you, my dear. How has your stay in the City been so far?" Emily pulled back to look her over.

"Interesting," Sara lowered her voice as her eyebrows rose ever so slightly. The women exchanged knowing glances for a brief moment.

"Hi, Mac," Sara said, looking over Emily's shoulder. The ever-present driver, Mac, was as much family as anyone and was still holding Emily's jacket.

"Good to see you, Sara," Mac replied as he handed the wrap to Emily.

"Head on home, Mac," Kyle said across the car. "Em and I will walk home tonight." Mac nodded and disappeared into the black sedan.

"Have you been here before, Carson?" Kyle began. "This is one of our favorite spots in town."

"Only once and loved it," Carson replied. "It's Sara's first time so she is in for a treat," he added while offering Sara his arm.

Kyle's favorite table overlooking the corner of 57th and 6th was ready and waiting, as was normally the case at least one night a week. Prior to being seated, Kyle had placed an order for a bottle of *Wilde Farm* Pinot Noir. Once the bottle arrived at the table, three glasses were filled with wine and one with sparkling water as Kyle offered the first toast of the evening.

"Our lives are better because she was part of them." He gingerly lifted his glass. "May her work continue through each of us, making the world a better place, one person at a time. To our dear friend, Clara." Four glasses ever so gently touched in the middle of the table, sealing a reverent moment of silence.

"Congratulations on the book, Carson," Emily lifted her glass again. "I couldn't put it down. Just when I thought there was nothing more to learn about my friend, she continues to surprise me."

Carson nodded in agreement.

"The tour has been bittersweet." He raised his glass of sparkling water in return.

"So, Sara. Have you given any thought as to what you are going to do now?" Kyle interjected across the table. Sara took a slow sip of her wine before she spoke.

"We continue to run the office until the special election can be held. The process can take up to six months as you know," Sarah said in a state of reflection. Once we have a new Representative, that person will choose his or her own staff. I guess, in six months, I could be looking for a job," Sara added.

"There is something I've been wanting to share with the both of you, but the timing hasn't been right," Kyle chose his words carefully. The statement brought both Sara and Carson to full attention. "A month before she passed away, Clara shared with me her intent to retire at the end of her current term," Kyle informed the now speechless table. "We were actually working together on a transition plan when she experienced her heart attack."

Sara reached for another sip of her wine as her mind raced back to that dark day. *How could she not have known this as Clara's Chief of Staff?* was the only thought she could manage. The delivery of dinner provided the much-needed mental break, allowing a flustered Sara to gather her thoughts.

"She never gave any indication during our time together," Carson offered as everyone prepared to eat.

"Clara was planning on making the announcement towards the end of the book tour," Kyle replied.

Sara regained her ability to form words and interjected, "Did she say why she was going to retire?"

"She had her reasons, but top of the list was her desire to pass the reigns to the next generation to take up the cause," Kyle explained. He turned and looked deliberately at Sara. "Sara, she was planning to speak to you about running for her seat in the House." A stunned table turned and stared at an equally bewildered Sara.

Warm blood quickly circulated through Sara's body, crawling up her neck and creating a momentary lightheaded sensation. She gently placed her knife and fork on the table, avoiding everyone's stare. Sitting quietly, she finally looked up at Kyle. Knowing the mass of thoughts rushing through her head, Kyle did his best to move the conversation into a slightly different direction.

"I told Clara that was too much to ask of you, given the intense media spotlight any candidate receives these days. I offered her a counter-proposal." Kyle's revelations held everyone at the table riveted to each new word he spoke.

"And what was your counter-proposal?" Emily asked, giving Sara time to catch her breath.

"That Sara could come work at Ellis International and have twice the impact, while avoiding the possibility of her public life splattered over every social media platform in the world," Kyle said while cutting the last piece of his steak. "However, this decision was always intended to be made by you, Sara."

Sara sat motionless, considering his words.

"Given the current timing of the special election, it would be quite the lift to get you in the race, if you are interested in filling Clara's seat," Kyle continued. "But, if that is what you ultimately want, Sara, I will put the entire force of the Firm behind you to make it happen," he offered in the calming tone for which he was famous. This was Kyle Ellis at his best. No one was a better leader and mentor, and no one could match his reputation in exclusive circles as *the kingmaker*.

Sara hadn't touched much of her food and was toying with her steak when Emily spoke up, "Enough shop talk. I think we have overwhelmed Sara enough for one evening." Emily gently placed her palm atop Sara's hand, coaxing Sara to cut into the main course.

Carson was unusually quiet for a reporter, disarmed of the never-ending list of questions he would normally ask in moments such as these. All he could think about was Sara's pensive expression and the Tiffany Blue ring box in the breast pocket of his jacket. The table conversation had dramatically altered the after-dinner conversation Carson had been orchestrating most of the day. For the first time since Clara's death, Carson was wishing he had more than the sparkling water to drink.

"Kyle, you never disappoint when we spend time together," Sara mustered her first words in several moments. "Just when I think I am impervious to surprise, Kyle Ellis pitches a curve ball to challenge my thinking."

"Here is what you need to take away tonight," Kyle gently coached. "Clara loved you dearly and had great hopes for your future. You also need to take away that you are not alone in your decision. You have friends here to support whichever direction you wish to go." Emily squeezed Sara's hand ever so slightly to reaffirm Kyle's words.

"Change was inevitable," Sara replied thoughtfully. "And I can thank Clara for her generous courage in, once again, connecting me to you. And to Emily," she smiled and squeezed Emily's hand in return. "Your support means the world to me. Thank you both."

Once the plates were cleared and the second bottle of wine emptied, Carson offered a moment of levity. "As a recovering journalist, I can safely say that I am tempted to fall off the wagon and write a sequel." His remarks brought a much-needed moment of laughter to the group. Sliding his chair away from the table, Carson looked at Sara. "I could use a walk in the park. You up for a post-dinner stroll?" Carson searched Sara's face, gauging her response.

"Em and I are also going to walk home if you want more company." Kyle pushed his chair back and folded his napkin on his plate.

"I think they have had enough of you tonight, my love," Emily said with a warm smile, leaning over to place a soft kiss on Kyle's cheek. She winked at Carson and Sara.

Sara's face answered Carson's question. Not wanting to add additional anxiety to the evening, he changed course with agility. "Actually, I just remembered. I have an early morning meeting with Abigail to review the last stop on the media tour," Carson said. "I'll walk you back to your hotel and grab a cab."

Sara's smile revealed her relief. As she stood up to slip on her coat, Sara was overcome with the thought of how much she had fallen for Carson Stewart. He wasn't the same person she first met years ago. Reaching to place her hand behind Carson's head, she stood on her tiptoes to brush Carson's cheek with a kiss. "Thank you for understanding," she whispered in his ear.

Back in her hotel, Sara drew a warm bubble bath. Sliding slowly into the water, she allowed her body to completely relax, relinquishing her tension beneath the white scented efferves-cence. With a glass of red wine in her hand, she leaned her head against the rolled-up towel, allowing the steam to sooth her anxiety. Each and every thought of the day slowly made its way through her exhausted mind. Exhaling deeply, Sara closed her eyes and quietly offered a prayer for wisdom.

The
DECISION

The sounds of *Imagine Dragons* thumped in Sara's earbuds as she made her way through the City streets en route to the park. At this hour, she shared the streets with the few other runners and dog walkers in the midst of their morning routines. Crossing 5th Avenue at 59th, Sara entered the park at the southeast entrance. Heading north on East Drive, Sara picked up her pace to shake off the morning chill. Her stride increased with each beat of the heart-pounding music reverberating in her ears.

As a former college athlete, Sara had always valued increasing her heartrate as the perfect cleanse for her mind. With the last 24 hours still consuming most her thoughts, she had decided upon a three-mile run as just the right medicine to begin her day. With the change of song came a slight change in pace. The slower speed allowed her heartrate to recover just enough for a light bead of sweat to form under her headband. Her thoughts were becoming clearer with each additional step. Checking her watch, she realized even with the slower pace of the new song, she was still running six-minute miles in the cold morning air.

Exiting the park at 69th Avenue on the West Side, she walked to Columbus Avenue to allow her heartrate to fully recover. Once at Columbus, she turned left, on a mission to Joe's Coffee shop-the alter ego to Uncle Joe's Bar in the Village. Pulling open the black winter door that was attached to the storefront during the colder months, Sara was greeted by the sweet smell of fresh roasted, whole bean coffee brewed to perfection.

"Drip with one Splenda, please." Sara rubbed her hands together as she approached the compact counter. Within moments she was presented with the fresh brew, which provided a comforting warmth to chase her post-run chill.

Finding a seat along the wall, Sara retrieved her phone from her running arm strap. Scrolling through her email, she came across a message from her Executive Assistant in the D.C. office. It was marked "urgent." Tapping on the message, she read the first sentence: Simon Sanders plans press conference for later this morning to announce his bid for Mrs. Becker's seat.

Sara immediately forwarded the email to Kyle with the message, *"We should discuss this. Call me when you can. Sara."*

Once Sara hit send, she grabbed her coffee and made her way through the crowd of people who had squeezed into the tiny coffee shop. Stepping onto Columbus Avenue like a pro, Sara waved down the first cab.

"Four Seasons," she said, balancing her coffee as she slid into the backseat. While reading the remainder of the email, Sara's phone vibrated. The screen indicated it was a call from Kyle Ellis.

"That was quick," Sara muttered while adjusting her earbuds.

"This doesn't surprise me at all. Clara and I suspected he would run once she announced her retirement. Simon has been developing quite the stir over the last several years," Kyle added.

"He was the one-person Clara struggled to speak about with kindness," Sara noted.

"That is no surprise," Kyle cut in. "Privately he made it abundantly clear he wanted Clara out. His business tactics were more than questionable. Clara had enough evidence to bring him before Congress and was measuring her response just weeks before her death," Kyle said. "Simon has his hands in more politician's pockets than any one super-pac."

"I just finished a run and am heading back to my hotel. We should connect if your morning permits," Sara said. "It would be good to debrief last night. Also, there is something else I need to share."

"Always time for you, Sara. I'll meet you at the office if that works. Just a short walk from your hotel," Kyle teased. Sara smiled ironically at Kyle's humor, given his office building was adjacent to the Four Seasons Hotel.

"9:30?"

"Perfect. See you then," Kyle replied as the call ended.

Exiting the elevator into Kyle's private lobby, Sara realized it had been several years since her last visit. Kyle appeared holding two coffees.

"Yours if you want it," he said, extending his hand.

"Thank you. My first cup this morning went to waste," Sara said, accepting the white ceramic mug from Kyle.

"Come on in." Kyle stepped aside, allowing Sara to lead the way into Kyle's office.

Not wasting any time, Sara produced the zip drive from her coat pocket and handed it to Kyle. Taking a sip of his coffee, Kyle carefully inspected the artifact.

"I'm guessing from Clara," Kyle offered, turning it over in his hand.

Sara nodded. "She left me a series of messages. I've only watched one."

Walking to his desk, Kyle placed the drive into the USB port of his laptop. With a remote control, Kyle changed the input on the 72" monitor on the opposite wall. With one click, Kyle's desktop appeared on the massive monitor. Clicking on the newly opened file, the password box appeared.

"The Great State of Texas, all one word" Sara said without any hesitation. "And, all lowercase."

Kyle laughed out loud, "Of course it is."

Sara's eyes scanned the entire contents once they appeared on the oversized screen. Her first look at the file on Joe's small laptop was much more restricting. Now with a full view, Sara could see the full extent of Clara's messages to her.

"I watched the first one with Joe yesterday," Sara began. She smiled as she continued, "Clara was always teaching. Even now, she is still teaching me."

Kyle carefully studied the dates of each recording. Scrolling midway down he double-clicked on one particular file. "This was the day after our first conversation about her retirement," Kyle said as he moved from behind his desk to take up a position next to the tufted leather chairs in the center of his office. He motioned for Sara to join him, and she slowly moved towards the open chair.

"Sara, there is something I want to talk to you about. I'm going to record this while it is fresh in my mind. It has come time for me to retire. Once my term runs out, I'm going to let someone else run for my seat. This is a lot to take in, but I am going to ask you to consider running and filling my position. I can't think of anyone more qualified to represent our great state than you."

Sara's eyes became moist watching her mentor address her, alive on the screen. Kyle quietly produced a tissue for Sara, which she graciously retrieved from his hand.

Clara continued, "I've spoken with Kyle and he is going to handle all the details of the election. With my backing, the race should be somewhat painless. Although, after two decades in D.C. I've come to acknowledge nothing is painless when it comes to this town. Simon Sanders is the only person who could pose a serious threat given his deep pockets; however, he shouldn't be an issue once he appears before the House to answer for his mounting unethical business dealings inside and outside D.C."

"Given the tight timing on the special election, maybe we should reconsider our thinking," Kyle Said. Sara shifted her weight in the chair to get a better view of Kyle.

"What made you change your mind?" Sara began and then stopped before she could finish her complete thought. "It has something to do with what Clara said, doesn't it?" Sara asked in a firm tone.

"It may be nothing. But you have to consider that without her backing, the race will be an all-out dogfight with you going up against a bottomless war chest of funds," Kyle offered in response. "If you want, we could put together an exploratory team to poll the District to see what we are up against."

Sara glanced at her phone to discover a missed call. "Carson called. I should call him back," Sara said in an effort to temporarily divert the conversation. "Give me a day to think this over. I'll have an answer for you then."

"Sara, my offer still stands. I could use a presence in Dallas, or you could work here in the City. Your call," Kyle offered as Sara stood to leave.

"Thank you, Kyle. You don't know how much that means to me," Sara said warmly.

Pulling the drive from his laptop, Kyle handed it back to Sara.

"Keep it," she said. "I copied it onto my personal laptop last night."

Kyle nodded and placed the drive in his pocket.

"We will speak tomorrow. If you needed anything, ring me." Kyle walked with her towards the elevator.

Once Sara stepped into the ornate lobby on the ground floor, she called Carson. "How's your morning?" Carson asked when he answered the phone.

"My morning run did me some good. That is, until I found out Simon Sanders is holding a press conference this afternoon announcing he is running for Clara's seat," Sara began. "I just left Kyle's office. He wants me to reconsider now that Simon is going to run."

"Good counsel given Sanders' deep pockets," Carson commented in a supportive tone. "I wrote a piece on him years ago. Not the most highly respected person inside the Beltway."

"Apparently Clara felt the same way. She was finalizing the subpoena to bring him before Congress on several of his nefarious activities." Sara switched gears. "Any chance you have time to discuss everything over a bite to eat?"

"I just wrapped up with Abigail. Early lunch?" Carson asked.

"That works out perfectly. Something I want to show you. Can we meet at the hotel?" Sara answered quickly.

"Sounds great. See you in 30 minutes," Carson responded with a hint of joy in his voice.

Sara took advantage of a few extra minutes of fresh air to gather her thoughts. Turning right out of Kyle's building, she made the decision to take a lap around the block to her hotel. As she walked, Clara's words about courageous generosity kept flashing through her mind. When Clara spoke about being generous with time and connections, was a campaign for public office what she had in mind? Consumed by her thoughts, it wasn't until she heard, *"Welcome back Miss Davis"* from the top-hat-clad doorman at the Four Seasons that she realized she had made it to her hotel.

Carson stepped out of the cab at the curb of the grand hotel, only to feel the pressure of the ring box still in his jacket pocket. Making his way through the lobby, he spotted Sara near the entrance of The Garden restaurant. Carson paused to take in Sara's beauty, looking at her as if it were the first time he had ever laid eyes on the stunning woman from Texas. Carson was so enthralled with her natural beauty that he never noticed Sara was carrying her laptop even as the hostess seated the two of them in the forest-themed room.

After ordering two sparkling waters, Sara produced her computer from her lap. "Something I want to show you," she began. "You may already know about this given you are the one who gave her the idea," Sara continued as she opened the laptop, placing it on the table for both of them to view. The laptop revealed the opened file folders of Clara's recordings.

"I wondered what she was up to," Carson murmured, simultaneously nodding his head while looking at the laptop screen.

****

Kyle slid into his desk facing his computer and typed an internal email to his Chief of Staff. "*In preparation for a possible Congressional election put together a deep profile on Simon Sanders. Top Priority.*" Kyle hit send to activate the well-connected resources of Ellis International. Kyle wanted to know what, if anything, Sara may be getting herself into should she decide to run for Clara's seat. He knew all too well that every election is filled with foul play since the merchandising of misinformation had become so commonplace that the country's general population had become numb to its effects.

****

"Have you given any thought to your decision?" Carson asked as he cut into his salad.

"Clara shared with me in her first video the idea of courageous generosity, being willing to get into the arena and dare greatly. Those words have been replaying over and over in my mind," Sara said, holding her water glass suspended mid-drink.

"The arena doesn't have to be politics you know. The same ideas could thrive within Kyle's group," Carson suggested in a tender voice. Sara smiled, setting the glass on the table, her eyes brighter than normal as she looked at Carson.

"That's what I love about you, Carson Stewart, always thinking."

Carson paused to take in the moment, feeling his heart race ever so slightly.

"I told Kyle I would have a decision by tomorrow," Sara said with finality.

"Whatever decision you make, we should celebrate at Joe's. Tomorrow night, 7:30," Carson said with determination.

"Done." Sara's smile widened as she continued. "Thought I might pop in on Abigail this afternoon."

"She would enjoy the break from the book tour mania," Carson said with assurance. "I will drop her a text to let her know you are stopping by." The two made their way to the front entrance of the hotel.

"Thank you for lunch," Sara said, kissing Carson as they exited to the street. "Brightest spot in my day," she added brightly, as the two walked with arms locked toward the 57th Street entrance of the hotel. Carson glanced at his phone.

"Abigail says, 'Brilliant' and 'looking forward your arrival.'" Replacing his phone Carson asked, "Can I give you a lift to her building?"

"Thank you, but it is too nice not to walk." Sara added an additional kiss to Carson's cheek. As the doorman held the door for Carson, Carson lingered for just a brief moment, absorbing all of Sara's beauty.

"Will I see you before tomorrow night?"

"I need to prep for a staff conference call in the morning," Sara replied.

"Then, tomorrow night it is." Carson feigned a pout, stealing one last kiss before disappearing into a yellow cab.

Standing in the foyer of the 6th Avenue tower, Abigail spotted Sara as she walked through the revolving doors.

"Sara!" A distinctly British accent reverberated across the crowed lobby. Looking towards the elevators, Sara spotted her friend dressed in a grey wrap coat with her long black hair draped perfectly over her collar. The extra height from her black high heel boots allowed Sara to easily spot her in the crowd.

"So very glad you came by. I so needed the break!" Abigail said as she reached out for a warm embrace. "We need coffee. I know just the place. Best kept secret in the City," she continued as she swept Sara into her arm as they walked toward the massive revolving door.

Once outside, they headed left around the corner of Rockefeller Center on 48th Street. The crowded streets kept the ladies close as they walked. "This is it," Abigail exclaimed as the two came to a very nondescript entrance at 1 Rockefeller Center. The heavy brass revolving door deposited the two into the lobby of one of the many towers in the art deco office complex. Flashing her security badge allowed Abigail and Sara access to the first bank of elevators. High atop the 36-story tower was a private space for tenants of the Rockefeller complex. Upon exiting the elevators, Abigail guided Sara down the long hallway towards the outside mezzanine deck overlooking the City on the East side of the building.

"Find us a place to sit while I grab two cups of coffee," Abigail said as Sara took a moment to take in the mesmerizing panoramic views of the City. Within minutes, Abigail reappeared with two coffees in hand. The soft white cushions in the deep wicker chairs provided a picture-perfect view of the City. The two friends sat back and relaxed while cradling their steaming cups.

"Carson filled me in on the highlights of dinner last night," Abigail began while gently sipping the hot beverage. "Seems you have a decision to make."

Sara nodded as she began slowly enjoying her drink as well. "What would you do?" Sara asked, peeking over the rim.

"Depends. I'd probably assess which position would provide me the most influence," Abigail said instinctively.

"Becoming a lawmaker seems to offer the pinnacle of influence," Sara said, drawing on her experience in the matter.

"Agreed, but isn't it true that even our representatives can be influenced, in both good and bad ways?" Abigail asked in a somewhat rhetorical fashion.

"True as well. So, are you saying you would not run for Congress?" Sara pressed.

"I'm saying that being a lawmaker can also lead people to depend on their authority as their tool of influence, a type of forced authority you might call it," Abigail explained thoughtfully. "It has been my experience that the real heroes are the people who can tap into the intrinsic motivation that moves people through their relational influence, not positional authority."

Sara silently pondered Abigail's words as she continued to sip her coffee. "Clara spoke often about the importance of our influence." Sara stared placidly at the skyline in the distance.

"When I work with authors, I'm frequently asked what I suggest they should write about," Abigail said with a grin.

Sara glanced quizzically back at Abigail. "True. Many ask what would sell the most books, and then they try to force their concentration there," she continued. "My counsel has always been the same over the years. Tell your story; focus on what is important to you and why it should be important to others. Write about how you are on purpose and others will desire to know more," Abigail pressed forward, solidifying a meaningful connection with Sara.

Sara leaned in with a chuckle, acknowledging the familiar words. "Oh my, you sounded just like Kyle Ellis at that very moment," Sara said, reaching forward to tap Abigail's hand. "And that is exactly the kind of person you want to sound like. I'm sold!"

They both shared an unpretentious laugh. Reclining into the deep cushions, they savored the final sips of coffee and the last, lingering moments of the majestic view.

The
PROPOSAL

Joe's Bar was packed to capacity when Sara arrived. The energy in the room was palpable as she made her way across the bar to the far corner where Carson was waiting. Marisa was the first to catch a glimpse of Sara as she squeezed sideways through the throng of people.

"Sara!" Marisa shouted in order to be heard over the energic buzz of the crowd. Hearing her name, Sara glanced at the bar and noticed Marisa pointing to Carson in his usual spot. With a wave of acknowledgement, Sara continued her short trek towards Carson.

"Where did all these people come from?" Sara asked as she greeted Carson with a kiss.

"Marisa has transformed this place into the City's hot spot since she started working here. Her enthusiasm and creativity is the best thing to happen to Joe in years." Carson leaned in close to be heard.

Out of nowhere, Joe appeared with a frosted glass and a bottle of Sara's favorite sparkling water.

"Great to see you, Sara," Joe said, his smile barely visible behind his thick beard. Sara returned the smile while removing her coat.

"Good to see you, too, Uncle Joe."

Skillfully pouring the sparkling water into the glass, he commented, "Seems you've had quite the eventful week."

"You could say that," Sara replied with a hint of exhaustion in her voice.

"Come to any conclusions?" Joe asked, never one to beat around the bush.

Sara reclined on the well-worn stool, drink in hand as she pushed her hair behind her ear. "I'm not ready to run for office," she said in a very satisfying tone.

Carson's face revealed relief as he pondered her words. As a syndicated political writer earlier in his career, he was keenly aware of the brutal weeks and months that she would have faced had she chosen to run.

"Doesn't rule out a future run for office. Just not at this time," Sara explained before taking a long drink of the cold water.

"Sounds like the right decision," Carson said in a supportive tone. "You going to take the job with Kyle?"

"If he will still have me."

Almost on que, from behind Sara, a voice responded, "I've already taken the liberty to print your business cards." Kyle pushed through the crowd with a huge smile, pulling Emily through the noisy throng. Sara turned to greet them, relieved by his surprise affirmation.

"This is a treat. A bit out of your neighborhood," Sara laughed.

"We were invited. I understand the best sparkling water in town is served here," Kyle nodded toward Joe with a grin.

"Did you bring Mac?" Sara scanned the bar only to spot him positioned close to the door where he could keep an eye on the entire room. Sara waved once she caught his eye. Mac smiled and returned the gesture.

"Congratulations on your decision. It feels right to me," Emily leaned in close to Sara.

"Thank you, Emily, that means a great deal to me," Sara replied softly. "I'll still be in D.C. until the transition post-election," Sara added, mostly for Kyle's benefit.

"No worries here. We can put some resources behind the transition if needed. Just say the word," Kyle offered in a reassuring tone.

"Carson, you are unusually quiet tonight." Emily moved toward Carson, noticing a fine bead of sweat forming along his brow. Placing her hand on Carson's back she leaned in close. "You okay?" she asked discretely.

With a gentle, less than reassuring nod, he reached into his pocket to produce the Tiffany Blue ring box out of sight of Sara. Emily's eyes widened, fully understanding why they had been asked to join everyone for drinks tonight. In a comforting move, Emily gave Carson a look of deep approval. She placed her hand over his, trying to calm his nervous shaking and the panic threatening to overcome him.

Slipping back toward Kyle while creating a natural backdrop for Carson, Emily placed her arm around Kyle, giving him a gentle hug. After years of marriage, Kyle knew Emily was trying to tell him something, so he paused his conversation. Joe sensed the moment had come. He had spent the last two hours keeping Carson calm after Carson arrived at the bar early to ask for Joe's permission to marry Sara.

Oblivious, Sara leaned against the bar to refill her glass of sparkling water. Carson moved closer, carefully placing the ring box on the bar in Sara's view. Sara turned towards the flash of blue and froze in wide-eyed surprise. Time stood still, the noise of the bar fading to silence and there was nothing present in Sara's mind except her ring finger, Carson, and the unmistakable blue box in front of her. Sara could feel each beat of her heart reverberate inside her chest as her breathing became deep and deliberate. Slowly, Carson opened the box to reveal the three-carat round stone set to perfection in a six-prong platinum setting. The brilliance of the diamond lit up the room, revealing a full spectrum of vivid colors glowing in the dimly lit bar. Carson nervously cleared his throat while those nearest looked on.

"There is something I've been meaning to ask you for some time now," Carson began, his voice unsteady with nerves. As though someone had suddenly turned up the volume, Carson's voice broke Sara's sound barrier, catapulting her back into the present moment. Looking into Carson's eyes, she witnessed something she had only seen once before, a gentle flow of tears cascading across his face. In an instant, Sara's tears intermingled with his as she threw herself into Carson's chest wrapping her arms tightly around him. The hug was a silent yes spoken with every fiber of her body. Not leaving anything to chance, Sara softly spoke, "Yes, Carson, Yes."

The applause spread like a tidal wave through the crowded bar as those in close proximity recognized and spread what was happening. Marisa had made her way from behind the behemoth of a bar to stand alongside Sara and Emily. Together they admired the brilliance of the simple, yet magnificent ring. Joe was the first to grab Carson's hand from across the bar to congratulate his old friend. Kyle followed suit while retrieving three Davidoff Double "R" cigars.

"I know that, traditionally, cigars are matched with babies. But this felt worthy of a celebration." Kyle handed Carson and Joe one of the perfectly rolled masterpieces.

Joe reached behind the bar to grab the bottle of *Pappy Van Winkle*, a cold *Topo Chico*, and three glasses. "Follow me gentlemen. I have just the place," Joe said in one continuous move. Carson glanced over at Sara for approval, hesitating for a moment to follow Joe. He immediately received a smile and a kiss in return.

"I love you, Carson Stewart. Thank you for a perfect evening," she grinned. "Now, go. Spend time with the boys. The three of us are heading to the Four Seasons. Call me later." Sara added another kiss, this time a more deliberate lingering kiss that prompted another round of applause from the raucous bar crowd. Carson hesitated to retreat with Joe and Kyle, enjoying every bit of affection from his future wife. The smile on Sara's face confirmed that this mission was accomplished.

"Go! Call me later. Love you," she said as she gently pushed Carson toward his friends.

The
ELECTION

Special elections rarely produce a large turnout and the election to fill Clara Becker's seat was no exception. The unfunded candidates were no match for The Metal of Honor, billionaire Simon Sanders' election machine. Privately, with glasses of rare whiskey in hand, an elite group of D.C. powerbrokers sat watching the anti-climactic results on television.

"Whoever said you can't buy your way into Congress never met Simon Sanders," a deep, crusty voice from the back of the room muttered. The collective groan of the remaining members of the group confirmed the remark. Simon Sanders would now become one of them, and they were skeptical that their circle could encase his ego.

They took another sip of whiskey, an unspoken gesture that confirmed their collective insecurity about this unvetted new member of Congress. Powerbrokers don't like wildcards showing up at the table. Inside the Beltway, self-interest was the daily deal and the hand everyone expected would be dealt. With Simon Sanders, there was an uneasy sense his game somehow transcended self-interest and sought more than the normal grab for power. Simon Sanders' demons were unfamiliar to the group, and they weren't fond of strangers.

Sara and Carson watched the acceptance speech from Sara's home in Dallas. Simon entered the expansive ballroom amidst cheers from the sparse crowd. He climbed the stairs of the platform and slowly walked to center stage, waving at supporters along the way. Behind the podium draped with a red, white, and blue campaign sign, Simon was impeccably dressed in his custom suit, red tie, and custom black cowboy boots. Looking the part of a stereotypical Texas Congressman, Simon began to speak with a slow deliberate drawl.

Sara effortlessly pointed the remote at the flat screen tv and pressed mute. "Don't need to hear any more of his rhetoric," Sara said with a hint of fatigue in her voice. "The crowd is surprisingly small considering the size of the venue his staff booked," she said with the wisdom of a political insider.

"What are you saying?" Carson asked.

"Paid staff in the room mostly. Doesn't appear to be much of a grassroots crowd there," Sara commented to herself, transfixed on the now silent screen. Leaning her head to rest on Carson's shoulder, Sara exhaled ever so slightly as Carson turned to gently kiss Sara's head.

"A new season awaits," he offered in an encouraging tone. Moving closer into Carson's arms, Sara let the last several months of tension release as they sat quietly together with only the light from the images of the television filling the room.

****

Kyle reclined in his high-back chair, feet propped upon his desk in the study of his penthouse apartment on the upper Westside. The views across the Park offered a priceless landscape, perfectly framing the windows of the pre-war building. One of the oversized computer monitors displayed the internet live stream from the local Texas news outlet covering the election results. The opposite monitor had multiple pages of documents displayed in layers that covered the entire screen.

Kyle's lead researcher was no ordinary investigator. Susan Hall was a black-hat hacker with the unmatched ability to expose information people attempt to hide. Reaching for his cell phone he typed out a text message to Mac.

"Deep profile on Sanders revealed a connection with an offshore drilling company in Cuba. Going to need your help to look into this."
"Been looking for a reason to pick up some cigars. On it," Mac responded immediately.

With a few clicks on his phone, Kyle sent Mac the information he would need to investigate what appeared to be a well-hidden resource inside the Sanders empire. Kyle's first thought was to question why Simon would go to such great lengths to conceal this connection. Pausing for a moment to refocus his thoughts, Kyle scrolled through his text messages until he came to his last text to Sara.

"Looking forward to having you officially on the team," Kyle's thread began.

"Thank you, Kyle. I'm excited to begin this new journey," Sara responded.

"You have learned from the finest person I've known. Rest assured, the best is yet to come." Kyle couldn't resist mentioning Clara Becker.

****

"Can I get you anything?" Sara said as she slowly released herself from Carson's arms.

"I'm good," Carson replied.

Sara found her way to the kitchen to retrieve her one carbonated indulgence, a real cane sugar Coke in a bottle. Snapping the cap off in a swift motion, she wandered to the cozy study in the Highland Park home where she grew up. Reclining in the overstuffed, cream-colored reading chair across from her desk, Sara picked up her iPad from the side table. Opening the home screen, she tapped on the photos icon to reveal the various albums she had created. At the top of the page was the album titled "Clara."

Gently pressing on the screen revealed the videos Clara had left Sara. Staring at the screen for several seconds, Sara tapped the next video in the series. Appearing on the display was Clara wearing her favorite University of Texas t-shirt. Realizing this video must have been recorded on a game day, Sara couldn't help but smile knowing she was with Clara later that afternoon.

"Sweetie, I've been thinking a great deal about happiness lately. Carson has me telling stories from earlier in my career-long before you and I met. I haven't smiled that much in years. When we were done for the day it dawned on me just how grateful I am for all I've experienced in life," Clara began.

The smile on Clara's face prompted a mirror image to appear on Sara's face as Sara sat curled up in her chair, Coke in one hand and iPad in the other.

Clara continued, "I am truly happy Sara. But here is what I've discovered. It's not all about the pursuit of happiness. Don't get me wrong, I am all for finding happy, but the cold hard fact is that 'life is messy.' We live in a world of broken people, with myself being chief of the all broken people." She continued with her signature laugh. "I'm learning my happiness is a by-product of living inside my purpose. When Carson completes the book, you will see a common theme throughout, which is not new information. We all desire meaning in life. Problem is, sometimes life it just downright unbearable at moments. I've tried my best to provide a model for you to find meaning in the midst of the messy. Collectively, every person has a responsibility to fulfill in life: a responsibility to be in the arena of this messy life and dare greatly, to serve others with courageous generosity, to live a life of honor and compassion. Sara, it's in the messiness of the arena that you find your purpose," Clara exclaimed with the level of passion Sara had seen countless times on the floor of the House. "Well, sweetie, that is all for now. I'm off to meet you to cheer our Longhorns on to victory. Love you, my dear friend," Clara said as she signed off with a wink.

Sara didn't notice the tears streaming down her face as she sat motionless holding the now darkened iPad. With one hand holding the Coke bottle, Sara used the other hand to wipe the tears from her face. Placing the iPad back on the side table, she took a well-deserved drink of the sweet, carbonated pleasure. With a quick check in the mirror to ensure there were no noticeable black mascara streaks on her face, she made her way back into the main area of the house.

"Everything okay?" Carson asked, realizing Sara had disappeared for an extended period of time.

"Yep. Hey, is there a football game on we could watch?" she asked, finishing off the last swig of Coke. The comment brought a relieved smile to Carson's face as he hit the *last* button on the remote, exposing that he had been watching a football game in Sara's absence.

"Move over," Sara gave him a friendly shove, while grasping for a bag of chips and another bottle of the ice-cold beverage that was chasing down her tears.

•

The
FIRST DAY

"Will you be joining us for breakfast, ma'am?" Came the friendly greeting from the impeccably dressed valet.

"Yes, thank you," Sara replied as she stepped out of her black Range Rover onto the cobblestone circle drive. Her high heel shoes made a delicate clicking sound as she entered the majestic lobby of The Mansion on Turtle Creek's exclusive restaurant in the heart of Dallas.

Sara was greeted by name as she entered the restaurant. "Miss Davis, your party is here. I will show you to Mr. Ellis' table."

Across the bright room, Sara followed the smartly dressed hostess to the sunroom. There, in the far corner, reading the local paper, sat Kyle Ellis. Sensing her arrival tableside, Kyle folded his paper and rose to greet Sara.

"Good morning, Miss Davis," he said cheerfully, emphasizing his friendly formality. "Welcome to your first day with Ellis International."

Sara smiled as she placed her Chanel handbag on the empty chair.

"Great to see you, Kyle," Sara replied with a strong, deliberate handshake and hug.

Once breakfast had arrived, Sara jumped into the conversation. "After several years of hearing Clara talk about you and your firm, I feel like I should know everything there is to know." Kyle smiled at the affirming comment. "We are a purpose-focused firm driven by our client's needs, correct?" she continued.

"You could say our purpose is our client's purpose," Kyle added as he sipped his coffee. Sara nodded in approval as she recognized where Clara got her version of the same statement.

"If you keep this one idea in mind, you will find success for your clients and for yourself." Kyle let his words hang for dramatic effective. After a pause long enough for him to take the last bite of his multi-grain toast, he continued, "You will find we have no power with our clients, so we rely on authentic-influence to lead."

Sara leaned in closer to the table in order to take in everything Kyle was saying.

Kyle continued, "There are two types of people you will come in contact with: The person who has been placed in a position of authority over others and those who have no authority. People who have been given power but are poorly equipped to lead will struggle. To get anything done, these people force their positional power onto the people they lead. We refer to this executive style as Forced-Authority." Sara nodded in agreement as Kyle's words confirmed what she had experienced for years in D.C.

"To serve our clients we need to help them move from a forced-authority model to a model of authentic-influence." Kyle leaned back into his chair. "We can discuss more about how to go about that once you get settled in." Kyle gave a gentle wave to the ever-present wait-staff for the check. "Now, we need to go check out our newest office space here in Dallas," Kyle continued while signing the check. "May I ride with you?" he added. "Mac is running an errand for me so I'm without a car."

Sara smiled, realizing this was the first time she had seen Kyle without Mac close by.

Once in the Range Rover, Sara navigated her way through the back streets of downtown Dallas like a true local. Just a few blocks from the hotel, Sara turned into the Uptown area of downtown Dallas. Circumnavigating through the underground garage, she came to a reserved parking space. Stepping into the lobby of the glass tower, Sara was overwhelmed with joy as the realization of her new career opportunities washed across her body.

"Welcome to Ellis International's Dallas office," Kyle said with an overt sense of pride in his voice.

The office reverberated with a strong, energetic vibe from the moment one entered the lobby. A team from the New York office had been in Dallas setting up the space and hiring talent for the last 30 days. Preparations to transfer a handful of strategic clients to the Dallas office were underway, with the focus on one key client in particular. Portman Technology was led by CEO, Monica Portman, a second-generation family member of the multi-billion dollar, privately held tech company. The transfer made strategic sense, given Monica and Sara attended law school together at SMU. Kyle had strong inclinations that this would be an excellent client match for Sara.

Sara stood in her new office overlooking the heart of Dallas. The well-appointed space had been designed by Dallas' top interior designer and fit Sara's personality perfectly. Each detail had been considered, right down to the silver framed picture on Sara's desk of her posing with Clara. Taking a seat on the cream-colored sofa, Sara reclined for the moment to reflect on the big changes in her life.

"Great space." Kyle stood in the doorway of the expansive corner office.

"Yes, it is. Thank you," Sara replied gratefully.

"I have to get back tonight. Portman Tech's Board meeting is next week in New York," Kyle said. "I've scheduled time while Monica is in town for the three of us to have dinner. She has hidden potential she has yet to discover-well beyond her role as CEO," Kyle added. "It is our role to help her find it." He retrieved his phone to text his pilot.

"I'm happy to give you a lift," Sara offered.

"No worries. With Mac out of town, I have our company pilot flying me home tonight. He is swinging by to pick me up on the way to the airport," Kyle said.

"Any final words of wisdom before you head out?" Sara asked, standing to see Kyle off.

"Our Firm is one of the top PR firms in the country. Your experience as Clara's Chief of Staff uniquely qualifies you to handle any situation you face. Don't second guess your talent. Be you," Kyle offered as the two headed towards the elevators. "There is more to what we do than PR," Kyle added softly, to avoid undue attention to the conversation. "I know Clara confided in you, so I can trust you." Kyle slipped into the elevator as the doors slid open. "I look forward to sharing more very soon." Kyle disappeared as the elevator doors closed.

Sara stood silently staring at the elevator, realizing what Kyle had been referring to all along. Clara had told her years ago about Kyle's secret talent helping people to unlock great potential on their way to the highest level of influence in the world. It now appeared the kingmaker had a protégé.

The
MEETING

Sara, back in New York, reclined in an oversized sweatshirt, one leg hanging off the edge of the king-sized bed at the Four Seasons, a cup of hot tea in her hand. Her laptop was opened on her lap as she reviewed page after page of documents in preparation for her meeting with Monica Portman the following night.

Monica was the oldest daughter of billionaire tech wizard, Martin Portman. Having grown up in Texas, Monica watched her dad build a tech company in Austin from the ground up before tech was even cool. Starting in his garage while still in college, Martin built with a simple philosophy: design usable products and make them available to the public at a fair price. This simple strategy ultimately garnered him billions.

Monica first met Sara in law school at SMU. At one point, they shared an apartment just off campus for a semester. There were many weekends where Monica and Sara found their way to Sara's home in Highland Park to have dinner with Sara's mom. Even at a simple dinner, Monica was always the prevailing personality in the room. Her ability to connect with people was gleaned by watching her dad interact with his employees at every level in the company. By the time Monica entered law school, her thoughts were focused on practicing law. Shortly after she passed the bar, however, her father was diagnosed with cancer. This news prompted a change in focus for both Monica and her father. The sickness slowed down the lively icon, eventually requiring him to step down from his daily duties as CEO and Chairman. While in remission, he seized the opportunity to further prepare Monica to take over as CEO. While remaining as Chairman, albeit at a much slower pace than years past, Martin continues to mentor Monica as she leads the multinational organization. Still single, Monica splits her time between the Austin headquarters and New York City where the company has been expanding its international operations.

Taking one last sip of her chamomile tea, Sara gently closed the lid of her computer. Placing the laptop back on her desk, she sat on the modern sofa in her room looking out at the brilliance of the City skyline at night. Reaching into her handbag she withdrew her iPad. Scrolling through different screens, she opened the video file for Clara. Pressing gently on the screen, the face of her dear friend appeared.

"Hi, sweetie," Clara began. "After today's interview with Carson, it really hit home how important character is. Admittedly, the longer a person stays in D.C. the more relative the word becomes. What I love about Carson is the way he made me unpack this big word. Of course, integrity plays a huge role in anyone's character. But I believe it is more than just integrity. There is a level of personal accountability that is involved. If we don't take accountability for our actions, we slip into chaos. Lord knows we have our share of that in Washington," she said with a laugh.

"You remember what I told you the first time you met Carson? Everyone deserves a second chance, even Carson Stewart. Sweetie, I believe our ability to forgive is as fundamental a part of our character as is our capacity to love others," Clara declared in a very matter of fact tone. "This is nothing you haven't heard me say before. Just wanted to get it recorded for you to always review. Heck, Carson is putting this in the book for all I know," she said with an immense laugh. "A strong character builds a resilient influence. Now, I have to run my friend." And with a wink, Clara was gone.

Sara placed the iPad back into her bag. Resting her head in her hand, she felt her eyes begin to get heavy. Pulling the massive sofa pillow close to her chest, Sara allowed the cushion to softly engulf her head. Her heavy eyes stared out the windows high above the City below. As she drifted off to sleep, the words of her longtime mentor rolled around in her mind. They idea of character impacting a person's influence was her final thought before she was overcome by complete REM sleep.

****

In the soft glow of the living room in Kyle's apartment, Emily had her feet propped up on Kyle's lap with her head buried deep into the opposite end of the sofa. Kyle caught a quick glance of Emily's hair cascading across her face as she drifted in and out of sleep. The light on Kyle's phone created an additional glow in the room along with a gentle vibration. Glancing over, Kyle noticed it was from Mac.

"Your suspicions were correct. He was hiding something," Mac wrote.

"Serious?"

"Off the books operation with Cuba," Mac reported back.

"Tax fraud?" Kyle was quick to respond.

"It appears so."

"Head home. We have work to do. Thanks, my friend."

Kyle stared thoughtfully at his phone.

****

Abigail and Sara started their morning run just as the early sun began to light the City. As they headed north on 5th Ave, their tightly pulled ponytails bounced in perfect rhythm with their morning pace. Even during the middle of the week, the City registered a peaceful hum as it slowly groaned awake. Glancing at her watch, Abigail realized they were on a serious pace for the three-mile run.

"You're pumped up this morning," Abigail said as a glaze began to form across her face.

"Sorry, just excited for the day," Sara replied without breaking stride.

"What has you so excited?" Abigail asked, keeping time with Sara's pace.

"Something Clara said in one of her videos I watched last night," Sara continued. "Clara made the connection between character and influence in her message to me."

With her breathing a bit more strained, Abigail replied, "Makes perfect sense."

"Earlier this week, Kyle discussed our firm's client approach: *authentic-influence* is our coaching methodology," Sara said, as she continued to connect the dots in her head.

Running down the stairs at the Bethesda Fountain, Abigail and Sara rounded the fountain and attacked the stairs back up to street level. Her heartrate close to her maximum, Abigail found herself wanting to slow the pace once the two were back on level ground. Sara's drive was unwavering as she realized her heartrate had reached full anaerobic capacity. Talking was more difficult at this point in the run so the two glided along in silence for the next several moments.

Heading south along The Mall, they directed themselves back towards 59th. Thankfully, the traffic light at 5th and 59th offered the first break in their morning run. Taking in deliberate deep breaths of the crisp morning air, Abigail and Sara allowed their heart rates to recover while they waited for the light to change.

"Follow me and I'll buy you breakfast," Sara said as she darted across the street, timing the changing of the light perfectly. Momentarily caught off guard, Abigail exclaimed, "Buggers!" and darted after Sara with a partial grimace and grin.

Flawlessly timing each light with their adjusted pace, both Sara and Abigail found the new stride allowed them to continue their conversation. For the next several blocks, they ran and continued to talk occasionally, zigzagging to avoid the early morning city dwellers. At 46th Street, Sara turned right and picked up the pace just enough for Abigail to notice and make the same adjustment. In a few long strides, Sara pulled up and gradually began to slow her sprint to a walk. With both hands on her sides, she deliberately walked towards the corner of 6th. Coming to stop at the corner, Sara pointed at an entrance.

"Here we are, breakfast!" she announced.

Panting and looking upward to determine where they had finished, Abigail scanned the building for a sign indicating where they were. Still breathing with deliberate effort, Abigail proclaimed, "Chick-Fil-A?"

Sara laughed at Abigail's overtly British proclamation. Tapping her watch, Sara scrolled through the screen to summarize the outcome of their morning run. "Eight-hundred calories. You need some fuel," Sara replied with a sly grin. At the counter, Sara ordered for the two of them. "Two chicken biscuits and two medium sweet teas," she said with the authority of a regular patron.

As the two claimed a spot along the glass wall facing 46th Street, they pulled up the red barstools to enjoy the crispy sandwiches.

"You know, a Brit drinking her morning tea filled with ice and sugar is quite the sight," Abigail said while taking a long draw on the straw. "You think I can get a refill?" she added with a wide smile of approval. The two laughed together, enjoying each other's company while the City came to life.

"I've been thinking about what you said earlier," Abigail began. "When Kyle talked about authentic-influence, what do you think he was referring to?"

Sara nodded while Abigail finished off her sweet tea. "Clara talked about influence as the true definition of leadership many times. She would say that influence is our ability to tap into another person's intrinsic motivation through connection."

"So why authentic-influence?" Abigail's inquiry made Sara fondly reminiscent of her talks with Clara.

"It is possible to be bad influence," Sara replied as they simultaneously burst into laughter. "Over the years in D.C. I've seen countless examples of counterfeit relationships being made with the sole purpose of personal gain. People using people to get what they want is sport in that city." After pausing for a moment to reflect on what she was explaining, Sara continued, "So, authentic-influence is built on the foundation of having the other person's best interests at heart. The best application of authentic influence is purposefully connecting with another person in an effort to help fulfill another's purpose."

Abigail leaned in to touch Sara's hand. "Well said," she agreed, her eyes affirming the wisdom in Sara's words.

****

Mac stood beside the black Mercedes and greeted Sara as she made her way out of the hotel.

"Good evening, Miss Davis," Mac said as he opened the door of the sedan.

Inside Kyle was reading a document on his tablet. Once Sara was situated in the backseat, he darkened the screen and placed the tablet between them. "Ready for tonight?" he began.

"Ready," Sara replied. "It's been several years since I've seen Monica so it will be great to catch up."

"Primary goal for the evening is just that," Kyle added as Mac made his way through Mid-Town Traffic. "When she debriefs the board meeting, listen for purpose moments," Kyle coached. "Those are the moments during a conversation where she connects to her personal purpose the most. Sometimes it's tone or an extended comment. The best case is when people deliberately proclaim, *this is it*!" Kyle offered with an immense smile.

As the car approached the restaurant, Kyle asked, "Have you and Carson picked a date yet?" The question brought a warm smile to Sara's face as she caught herself gently caressing the solitaire ring on her finger.

"Next June, in Hawaii, if he has his way," she said with a smirk.

"I'm guessing you were hoping for a Dallas wedding?" Kyle responded. Sara's smile confirmed Kyle's observation as Mac opened her door.

Kyle and Sara walked into the tall, black doors of the One57. At 90 stories high, it stands as one of New York City's tallest residential towers. Entering through the private residential entrance, Kyle and Sara made their way to the 84th floor. Portman Technology held their quarterly board meeting at the Park Hyatt New York, which occupies the first 30 floors of the soaring glass tower overlooking the City. Given that Monica retained her City apartment in the building, the convenient location was made available to the company.

"Monica, it is so good to see you!" Sara exclaimed as she entered the foyer of Monica's apartment. Monica's warm embrace was more symbolic of old friends than business colleagues. Sara's mind drifted back to their first year of law school, spending endless hours in baggy sweatshirts, ponytails, no makeup, all while consuming copious amounts of coffee studying for the next exam. The exhaustion was real as was the bond built during the early morning hours when delirium turned to giggles turned to moments of vulnerability, sealing their friendship for all time.

"Sara, it's been too long, my friend," Monica smiled, her demeanor energized by the sight of Sara. She drew Sara closer to her and whispered, "When I heard about Clara, I should have reached out. My heart was broken, and I should have been there for you." Sara's eyes grew moist at the sincere sentiment.

"Thank you, Monica. That truly means a lot," Sara replied with compassionate appreciation.

Turning to Kyle, Monica placed a friendly kiss on his cheek. "Once again, you have performed to perfection adding Sara to the team." Monica pulled back with a sparkle in her eye. "Could be the best addition since we became a client," she continued.

"Thank you, Monica," Kyle replied with satisfaction. "We are extremely proud to have her on board."

"Come in and relax." Monica extended her arms, guiding the two into the comfortable, well-appointed space with the satisfying ambiance of home. The main living space revealed the impressive floor-to-ceiling windows nearly 1000 feet above the City below. The view of the City at night was breathtaking, and once again, Sara paused to take it all in.

"Spectacular, isn't it?" Monica said, alongside Sara as they both relished the view. "Can I get you something to drink?" she continued, moving towards the bar. "After today, I'm going to need something a bit stronger to start the evening." Monica turned to the staff members who were assisting with dinner. "Martini, dirty with three olives, please," she ordered.

Sara smiled and nudged Kyle, "Make that two."

Kyle chuckled and held up his hands. "You'll forgive me if I don't make that three. I'll go off the menu and order a Maker's neat, please."

"Sounds like the board meeting was interesting," Sara began before the drinks arrived.

"The company is doing very well; the board is happy," Monica said.

"Then what happened to evoke an order for a three-olive martini?" Sara nudged as if the two were still in law school together and blowing off steam after an exam. Kyle observed their casual banter, confirming he had made the right call by assigning Sara to take the lead with this client relationship. Their instant bond was transparently genuine from the first moment they walked in the door. The three settled in the comfortable seating area nestled in the corner of the space, which faced north towards the Park.

Authentic connections create authentic influence, he thought, as he listened carefully to the unfolding conversation.

"By every measure, the business world has confirmed the success our company is delivering. Personally, I have more than I could ever desire," Monica's voice trailed off ever so slightly.

"I sense a *but* coming," Sara interjected into the conversation. She simultaneously leaned forward, recognizing a potential purpose moment.

With a martini in hand, Monica relaxed with a smile. "That is what I loved about you in law school. You have this uncanny ability to read a person," Monica became thoughtful. "Yes, there is a *but*. With all this so-called success, for some reason I can't identify, I still feel something is missing," Monica confessed, taking her first sip of the martini.

Removing the stick of olives from her drink, Sara leaned closer to Monica. "This is what we call a purpose moment," Sara waved her stick of olives. Kyle silently observed his young protégé, and with growing pride realized her abilities even eclipsed his expectations.

"A purpose moment? Do tell," Monica prompted.

"This is a great example of a moment which presents an extraordinary opportunity to connect to a person's unique purpose," Sara explained. "You are acknowledging that your business is enjoying great success. But, what I also understand you saying, is that you are not relishing this satisfaction on a personal level. What is it you find most satisfying about your work?" Sara continued.

Monica placed the now empty martini glass on the marble table in front of the sofa. She spoke thoughtfully, "I enjoy hearing how our products make a difference in the lives of the people we serve."

Sara's expression masked growing excitement. "Unpack what you mean by *'people we serve,'*" Sara prodded while using the olive stick as a pointer.

"My entire life, Dad coached me that we are here to serve, not to be served. Anything we do should be for the greater good of society. The financial bottom line was never Dad's primary focus," Monica began. "Developing products to improve lives is our purpose."

Sara listened to every word Monica said, thoughtfully processing Monica's father's instruction before she spoke again.

"Based on what you have told me about your father and the heart of this business, do you feel there is more to your purpose than creating and selling products?" Sara deliberately chose her words.

Kyle quietly placed his glass on the table, careful not to disrupt Sara's prompting towards a critical purpose moment.

Monica sat back in her chair and moved her gaze towards the City. Softly she replied, "That's always been it, Sara. My purpose is bigger than the products we sell and the financial reports that measure success. But I still haven't put my finger on my personal focus. How do I uncover that answer?" She turned back towards Sara and Kyle.

"Sometimes these answers are a natural consequence of asking the right questions," Sara began. "We have found that choosing the question is just as critical as arriving at an answer. There are two questions I want you to consider over the next few days that I believe will lead you to your purpose. Once you have spent some time in quiet reflection, we can connect and discuss what you came up with," Sara instructed.

"That sounds effective and appealing. What are the questions?" Monica asked, intrigued by Sara's guidance.

Sara held up her index finger. "First, what is the story being told about you today? Second, what is the story you want told about you beyond your resume?"

Sara allowed Monica a moment to absorb her words. Monica nodded as she processed the two simple questions. As she thoughtfully turned each question over in her mind, she slowly began to recognize the enormity of their breadth. The questions sounded simple, but arriving at an answer would require some soul-searching.

Kyle remained speechless, a silent witness of true leadership in the making. The patience Sara exhibited by introducing Monica to the process of unpacking her greater purpose was an exciting moment. Clara would have been so proud of Sara and her wise counsel. Kyle contemplated the words of Victor Frankl, whose insight eloquently acknowledged mankind's need to find meaning in life, even in the midst of suffering. While bearing the great tragedy of losing Clara, there was a greater leadership shift beginning to rise in Sara, which was directly inspiring Monica. How he wished Clara was here to experience Sara at the beginning of an exciting new season of her life. Kyle sighed deeply at the enormity of the moment and held his emotions in check until he could safely share the experience with Em.

While slipping on their coats at the end of the evening, Monica wrapped Sara in the warm embrace of friendship. Quietly she whispered, "God has placed you here for a moment such as this. Thank you for helping me refocus my purpose."

Sara squeezed her friend tightly as the two lingered fondly in grateful reunion.

The
DEAL

Simon Sanders proudly displayed his West Point ring as he conquered the halls of the Longworth office building in Washington D.C. As an infantry Captain in the Gulf War, Sanders served on the front lines as the coalition forces invaded Iraq. His service had proudly earned him The Metal of Honor, and his bravery was intoxicating to the press upon his return from duty. Every major publication vied to tell the story of his heroics after his squad came under attack during a classified mission, and Simon single-handedly eliminated the hostile force while saving the lone survivor of the ambush by carrying the wounded solider over three miles to safety.

After his tour of duty, with his newly fashioned fame, Simon worked as a private contractor with the Kuwaiti government, fueling his quest to become a major player in oil security and production. He leveraged his international fame into lucrative contracts that propagated his production operations stateside, expanding his empire into a multi-billion-dollar global oil powerhouse. His reputation as a shrewd and ruthless businessman preceded him as he tirelessly acquired most of his competitors for pennies on the dollar. The only city he had left to dominate on his quest to conquer the world was Washington D.C.

During the first few months of Simon Sanders' tenure in the House of Representatives, he conducted himself with the prowess of a senior member rather than a first-year freshman. It was quickly apparent that his reach and power had arrived in Washington long before he did. Working with military precision, he closed hallway deals with major players on both sides of the aisle. With the finesse of a chess grandmaster, Simon was quietly strategizing his game plan. Slowly and methodically he complied damning information on key leaders to leverage when the time was right.

If Simon's record in business was a precursor to his dealings in Congress, then his colleagues should have been alert to his proclivity to position any law necessary towards advancing his interests alone. Simon's tactics in business were uncompromisingly singularly focused: to win for himself and no one else. His tenure as a lawmaker was shaping up to be no different.

****

"How was dinner?" Sara received a text from Abigail.

"Wonderful."

"When are you back in town?" Abigail inquired.

"Two weeks. Coming up to see Carson☺" Sara's emoji depicted her growing excitement.

"Morning run?" Abigail pressed.

"Wouldn't miss it." Sara was relieved, anticipating some much-needed exercise.

"Great…need a sweet tea!"

Once settled into her seat in 4A, Sara placed her Sony noise-cancelling headphones over her ears to drown out the hum of the jet engine. Normally, she didn't mind chatting with her seatmate, but today she needed the three-hour flight to decompress and get a bit of work done before her weekend with Carson. Removing her iPad, she revisited the videos from Clara, relishing a few minutes of wisdom before she was consumed by her custom playlist and emails.

"Hopefully, you marry this man!" Clara opened with a sudden burst of energy. "We just finished a major milestone in the writing process. I must say, the more I get to know the real Carson Stewart, the more I like him. And I'm pretty sure you agree with me."

Sara's face began to glow as she concealed the screen, sinking deeper into her seat like a fidgety school girl.

"Today was one of those significant moments that really tipped the scales for me," Clara continued. "You and I have talked about the importance of significant moments when they occur. If we are not diligently present, we miss them and forfeit the vital message that would have been gleaned from the experience. We lose out on the ability to connect, which in turn, minimizes our influence. These moments don't happen often, but when they do, we need to be keenly aware of how we can apply what we learn to better serve those around us." Clara gazed reflectively at the screen. "When you get the chance, ask Carson about today's session. He will know what you are talking about when you refer to the chapter on listening." Clara ended with her signature wink as the screen went dark.

Sara closed her eyes and let Clara's words wash over her. Considering the last several weeks, she wondered how many significant moments she might have missed. Taking a mental inventory, Sara pulled out her journal and carefully began recording each significant moment she could recall during the last few weeks. Giving each event a title, she then wrote a sentence highlighting what she learned about the person or persons in each scenario. Then, she conscientiously recorded what she learned about herself. Once she had assessed herself and others, she concluded with one sentence summarizing her active leadership changes going forward.

Accompanied by a travel playlist, which consisted of music from Ben Rector, Elton John, Train, and others, she comfortably blocked all distractions and immersed herself into a deliberate space of focused thought. She scribbled a note in the margin of her journal: *Finding time for considerate contemplation is an important part of a balanced life.* Circling this sentence multiple times, she wrote next to it, *Make time to do this!*

Within minutes of adding the exclamation point to her thoughts, the wheels of the Boeing 737 touched the runway at LaGuardia Airport in New York City. Glancing out her window, she caught a glimpse of the majestic City across the river as the pilot slowly guided the plane towards the terminal. Retrieving her phone, Sara texted Carson to alert him of her arrival.

"Just landed. Will grab a cab and see you soon," Sara tapped.

"Great. See you soon." Carson's response appeared immediately.

Walking through the crowded terminal, Sara pushed through a diverse international cross-section of people, all maneuvering in a small confined space. As Sara came into close proximity with international travelers, she recognized that they all shared the commonality of searching for meaning and purpose in their lives. Scanning the long corridor, Sara was overwhelmed by the mass of humanity surging around her and felt a sudden sense of concern. *How can one person make a difference in such a vast world?* Her thoughts sought to betray her earlier convictions recorded in her notebook. Shaking off her sense of panic, she tightened her grip on her luggage and moved with the masses towards the escalator.

With one hand on her rolling luggage and her other bag hanging from her shoulder, Sara stepped off of the escalator onto the lower portion of the terminal and looked for the signs pointing to the taxi stand. Turning, she almost collided with a person whose face was concealed by a large white sign. It was emblazoned with the words, *"Welcome to New York City, Sara."* Sara stopped in her tracks, recognizing her name and the hasty penmanship. Lowering the sign, Carson stepped forward, holding a single rose. Sara gasped with surprise.

"Too cliché?" Carson asked with an innocent smile.

Sara returned the smile and silently closed the gap between them, embracing Carson with a full-strength clench, while burying her head deeply into his chest. Her soft whisper was barely audible.

"It's the perfect cliché."

Once settled in the waiting car, Carson reached over to hold Sara's hand. The soft touch of his fingers slowly wrapping around her small hand sent an electric shock through her body. She realized that each moment with Carson confirmed their commitment and brought their hearts closer together. Long gone was the overly narcissistic prodigy who had been stripped naked before his peers in a professional collapse of ethics and integrity. Sara had witnessed Carson at his absolute low point, prompted by an alcohol-induced suicide attempt. She also experienced the power of reconciliation in his life as he climbed out of rock bottom to the heights of restoration and regeneration. Sara had observed Clara personify her own words of courageous generosity when she came to Carson's aid, even after he had tried to publicly assassinate her character in the media.

For Carson, the unfolding plot for him to take the fall using misinformation had driven him to the brink of despair. He ultimately realized he had lost all hope and meaning in life. It was the compassion of Clara Becker that revived his faith in living. Her influence changed Carson to the core. He began viewing life through a different lens, understanding there was meaning within his struggle. Working with Clara to write her life story was an extension of his continued healing process. By recording Clara's words of wisdom, Carson began to really see Sara through a new lens. Clara's words, unveiled through his pen, inscribed onto his own soul the true meaning of love and honor.

"I made dinner reservations for us. We can drop your bags at the Four Seasons and head that way if you are up for it," Carson said with loving concern in his voice.

"I am famished, so dinner sounds great." Sara gave Carson's hand a gentle squeeze. "Where are we going?"

"I thought we could sprinkle a bit of Texas into your trip," Carson grinned. "Made us reservations at Del Frisco's."

Sara squeezed Carson's hand even tighter at the sweet gesture. "Perfect!"

Entering the expansive restaurant on the 49th street side of 6th Avenue, Sara felt at home in the luxuriously appointed space, full of deep wood and soaring ceilings. Above the wraparound bar, the words, *Be right and fear no man* called a bold greeting to entering guests. The young hostess greeted Carson and Sara promptly and escorted them to a prime spot on the upper balcony dining area. They paused for a moment to soak in the always busy crossroads of Rockefeller Center across the street and Times Square behind them.

"Two sparkling waters with lime for starters," Sara ordered cheerfully as the waiter stopped by their table. Carson smiled and nodded in agreement. Without looking at the menu, Sara was already prepared to order. She leaned into Carson, placing her hand upon his and smiled, "In case I forget later, thank you for a picture-perfect evening."

"You deserve a lifetime of these evenings," he replied, gently kissing her hand and gazing gratefully into her eyes. "We have so much to catch up on." He leaned back, keeping her in full view. "You first."

Placing her napkin in her lap, Sarah leaned back and returned his gaze. "Clara's latest video said I should ask you about your conversation with her concerning the topic of *listening*."

Carson smiled, his face alight with recognition. "I thought she might prompt you to inquire about that. You might recall that *listening* was the background framework of chapter four in the book."

Sheepishly, Sara began to fidget in her chair, awkwardly evading the fact that she had yet to read Carson's book. Observing her discomfort, Carson quickly caught on.

"Forgive me. It is understandable that you haven't read the book yet. The memory of Clara is still too fresh. I completely understand how you feel." He paused with emotion. "Honestly, Sara, it's painful for me each time I sign a copy as I so wish she was there with me to share in the experience." He continued carefully, "There is plenty of time to read it if you want to read it in the future."

Sara smiled sheepishly, grateful for his understanding.

"In that chapter, I asked Clara to identify and verbalize the most important skill for future leaders. Without blinking, she answered, *empathetic listening.*" Carson closed the menu resolutely, having made his final choice for dinner. Placing their dinner order with the hovering waiter, he continued, "*Listening with empathy* is at the heart of every significant moment we generate for other people."

Sara nodded in agreement, recalling the list she had made on the plane. *Make time to listen,* would definitely become her next entry.

"There are three parts to empathetic listening," Carson explained. "First, listening to what is being said. Clara indicated that she often used the key word *method.*"

"She discussed this with her staff frequently," Sara smiled as she replied. "She would instruct that when we listen for key words that people say, it keeps our focus on them, not us."

"Precisely," Carson nodded in agreement. "Next, Clara indicated it was important to listen for what was *not* said. I thought this was a bit odd until I took the time to consider it further and understood the important distinction. Our non-verbal language can be extremely expressive if we know what to look for." Sara gave Carson a look of confusion. "For example, your expression of uncertainly right now is communicating loudly," Carson smiled and continued in an upbeat tone. "Our body language and vocal tonality tell stories that are, at times, missed by others."

"Often, the process of listening to Clara's instruction included meditating on more than her words after she stopped speaking," Sara said quietly.

"Exactly," Carson nodded. "That reflection amplifies the last element of empathic listening. The key to empathetic listening is determining the real narrative being communicated, both verbally and *nonverbally*. Listening with empathy places you in an active learning mode and enables you to resist the impulse to give an immediate, uninformed response."

Sara remained silent with contemplation as she weighed Carson's words. "So, generating a significant moment is truly incubated by empathic listening?" she spoke tentatively, measuring each word.

"Exactly," Carson replied, finishing off his sparkling water. "She called it her common-sense list." Carson nodded his approval as fresh salads were placed on the table.

"Common-sense list?" Sara questioned, recognizing the opportunity to dig deeper.

"It emerged as we talked. Clara revealed that over the years, she had created a short list of basic, common-sense principles she lived by personally and professionally," Carson said with a chuckle, noting Sara's intrigue. "In her exact words, she lamented that 'common-sense wasn't common anymore.' Then she asked me if I had my own list," Carson grinned as he cut his salad into bite-sized portions. "She felt everyone should have their own list to keep them grounded to some basic common-sense ideas. And the more I have thought about it, the more I agree."

"So, I would guess that would mean that a couple items on Clara's list would be *courageous generosity* and *empathetic listening*," Sara said with growing confidence, her salad fork paused in midair.

Carson nodded in agreement, finishing the last bite of salad. He dabbed his mouth, placed his napkin on the table and thoughtfully folded his hands. "And you can also guess that those items have made their way onto my list too."

****

Snow began to blanket the benches in the park as Sara and Abigail jogged along the tree-lined path.

"The City is beautiful on mornings like this," Abigail panted as her heartrate began to rise.

"Not something we see in Dallas every year," Sara replied as she settled into her pace.

"Before I forget," Abigail cut in, "I may have a lead for a client."

"Really? Thanks. I appreciate that Abigail. What are the details?"

"One of my authors is a board member for a high-growth software company in Dallas. Seems the CEO needs some help as they prepare to go public. Thought it might be something you would be interested in pursuing." Abigail paused to catch her breath.

"Sounds intriguing. Why a PR firm?" Sara responded, her elevated heartrate making it more difficult to speak.

"Well, the CEO has no filter, internally or with the public. He is what you would call a hot mess." Abigail gave Sara a crooked smile.

"Sounds like the perfect conversation over a cold sweet tea." Sara returned the smile. "Biscuits and sweet tea. Now *that* makes this snowy run worth it!" Abigail added as the two gently picked up the pace.

****

Allen Bauerman began his business, Bauerman Group, ten years ago with the dream of becoming a publicly traded company. His software firm had enjoyed a double-digit rate of expansion each year for the last five years, garnering notable accolades in the marketplace.

Allen's reputation was best described as an autocrat. His high intelligence and low tolerance for people produced a condescending leadership style, resulting in an extreme *command and control* culture. To make matters more interesting, Allen had no reservations spending time and energy publicly bashing his competition, as well as his own employees, on social media with no regard for the consequences. With the continual loss of key members of his executive team, investors had cooled on the idea of infusing more capital for growth. No capital equaled no growth, which in turn equaled no IPO. It was that simple.

It was during an exit interview that a member of Allen's executive leadership team first pointed out the detrimental impact his leadership style was imposing on the business. In predictable fashion, Allen was able to manipulate the facts to falsely implicate the people surrounding him as incompetent. In Allen's narcissistic mind, without his leadership, the entire organization would collapse.

Finally, a prominent Board member, speaking on behalf of multiple other members, pulled him aside and issued an ultimatum. Allen was challenged to either procure external help or personally explain his intimidation tactics to Wall Street power-brokers who were increasingly concerned at the resignation of multiple high-profile board members as he tried to list his IPO.

Allen faced the toughest decision of his career, the lingering question, could he make the change required to lead his company to the next level.

The
LUNCH

Sara pushed the old wooden door open to enter a very crowded Joe's Place. The lunch crowd had consistently increased since Marisa had entered Joe's life. The simple menu combined with high quality food made the picture-perfect lunch hangout for the locals. Once inside the door, Marisa called out from behind the bar, "He's downstairs! I've got him working the kitchen." She waved, wearing a wide mischievous grin.

Heading down the narrow back stairs of the century-old building, Sara found Joe with Arthur and Patterson, placing the final touches on a successful lunch rush.

"Pull up a chair and we'll fix you a burger!" Joe wiped his hands on the towel hanging from his back pocket.

"Pink or no pink?" Arthur shouted from behind the grill, not missing a beat.

"No pink, please," Sara responded, sinking into the nearest ladderback chair.

The small television attached to the low ceiling was tuned uncharacteristically to CNBC. A condition of Joe spending time with both Arthur and Patterson was that they improved their business skills while they worked for him. CNBC never failed to generate an endless stream of questions from the two men. Sara glanced up at the scrolling newsfeed below the midday programming. Her eyes immediately caught the mention of Congressman Simon Sanders co-sponsoring a bill that would greatly benefit international oil companies. This news sent energy-related stock prices dramatically higher on the day.

Sara caught a glimpse of Patterson's reaction as she read the news. In a low, nearly inaudible voice, Patterson grumbled, "Some things never change."

Sara continued to stare at her, studying Patterson closely as the Gulf War veteran paused to watch the news with great intensity. Sara's concentration was finally broken by Joe as he dropped the hot, juicy burger in front of her. The fragrant aroma filled her nostrils, enticing her to redirect her attention to the red basket filled to the brim with a juicy burger and fresh cut fries.

Joe pulled up an old wooden chair, turned it around backwards, and straddled the seat. He leaned on the back of the chair and waited for her to take to dive in. Sara could now sense Arthur and Patterson jointly following his gaze, all anticipating her enthusiastic review of the lunch. Taking the burger carefully into both hands, she first noticed the freshness of the bun, encapsulating the perfectly grill-smashed burger patty. The smell was intoxicating, sending a wave of saliva to the back of her mouth in anticipation of the first bite.

"How's the burger?" Joe asked as Sara squeezed on the fresh bun to ensure the pile of condiments would not escape out the backside of the culinary masterpiece.

Waiting to partially chew her food, Sara replied with her wide eyes and over-stuffed mouth, "Love it." She covered her partially full mouth as she spoke. The team nodded in satisfaction as Patterson appeared at her elbow with a stack of much-needed napkins for one of the juiciest burgers in the City.

"Thank you," Sara mumbled as she wiped her mouth, swallowed and then carefully placed the napkin in her lap. Putting her hand on Patterson's arms, she restrained her from retreating back to the kitchen. "So, Patterson, tell me your story," she continued.

Patterson was frozen with the thought of having to speak.

"No story, ma'am. Just thankful for Joe," she said with a smile as wide as the Mississippi. Joe nodded in affirmation.

"We are thankful for you, too."

Patterson blushed, backing away with a deeply satisfied nod and smile.

"Patterson is much too modest," Joe remarked respectfully. "She served our country proudly and is now humbly making a difference in the lives of each person who enters this place," Joe continued as her blush deepened at the praise.

"Freakin' war hero, that's what she is!" Arthur shouted as he cleaned the grill with passionate energy. Joe looked at Sara's kind affirmation, her head nodding while she clearly listened to each man.

Patterson's head dropped as she grabbed his dish tub and scurried up the stairs to clear tables. As she disappeared up the narrow stairway, Joe leaned further over the back of his chair.

"Bethany Patterson was on a classified mission with her squad when her team was ambushed. As the team took cover, a sniper opened fire, taking out several of the team members and pinning down her Captain. Patterson caught a round in the shoulder before she was able to take out the sniper," Joe explained.

Sara was frozen, virtually unblinking as Joe continued to tell the story. "Much of the mission is still classified and Patterson doesn't talk much about the details. She saved multiple lives that day, yet the experience hit her hard. She discharged once she recovered from her shoulder wound and her tour was up. Sadly, the mental wound has yet to heal," Joe whispered with a tone of true concern. "When Marisa and I found Patterson at the shelter, she was homeless and unable to cope with the world. Here, she has been welcomed into a safe environment, working with a team, which gives her great purpose. My hope is that this has become a place of healing, allowing her to re-enter the world on her own terms."

"We'll get her through it," the gruff voice of Arthur chimed in from his spot behind the grill. Joe nodded and rested his chin on the back of the chair.

Sara sat motionless, holding her burger in mid-bite as she reflected on Joe's words. Placing her half-eaten lunch into the red basket, she looked at Joe cradling his chin in his hands.

"Patterson is proof that there are quiet heroes all around us if we would just take the time to learn their stories." She sniffed to compensate for the moisture building in her eyes. "Thank you for telling me her story."

Joe smiled as he stood and kissed Sara on the head. "That's what I love about you, kid. You really listen. And you always recognize the good in everybody."

As Sara made her way up the back stairs to the bar, Marisa paused while pulling a draft beer with both hands. "He misses seeing you, darlin'. Thank you for coming by and joining us for lunch."

Sara smiled, noticing Patterson out of the corner of her eye. Sara worked her way to the section where she was clearing and cleaning the tables.

"Did Joe happen to tell you I was some kind of hero?" Patterson asked with suspicion, never taking her eyes off the table she was cleaning.

"He did, and then some, Bethany," Sara replied in a gentle voice. Patterson's head darted up at the pronouncement of her first name.

"He's the real hero," Patterson said, as she slowly stood up straight.

"I think there are two heroes in that kitchen, Bethany," Sara said as she extended her hand. "Maybe three."

Slowly, Patterson extended her hand while Sara encased it in her own. She gently squeezed her rough palm.

Sara continued, "I used to work for one of the greatest members of Congress this nation has ever known. She would remind me often that her job was to make the laws, but the real heroes are the ones who stand in the gap to uphold our laws and protect our way of life. She told me time and time again that the real heroes are often found in the arena, their actions a substitute for a lifetime of words. I hope to share your arena and be a hero like you one day, Bethany."

Sara gave Patterson one more squeeze, released her grip, and turned towards the door. Before Sara could disappear into the fast pace of the City, she heard a voice, "Just call me Patterson." Sara turned toward Patterson. "And, ma'am."

"Yes?" Sara responded.

"Thank you, ma'am."

Sara smiled a deep satisfying smile as she looked upon the strong woman before her. "You are welcome, Patterson."

The
CLIENT

Sara stepped into the atrium of the historic pre-war building on the edge of the Dallas Central Business District. The old building had a retro feel with exposed wood beams, polished concrete floors, and open expansive spaces filled with adjustable workstations. Several head-phone clad employees stared intently at multiple flat screen monitors, filling the room with a steady drone of typing in countless lines of code. The only office walls were constructed in the corner of the mezzanine level of the open space. Towering over the employees below, Allen Bauerman stood at his raised desk staring at a portion of the Dallas skyline.

Sara's heels made a distinctive unnatural sound in the casual office environment. As she entered Allen's office, his assistant announced Sara's arrival.

"Miss Davis is here to see you, Mr. Bauerman," the intimidated assistant said in a diminutive monotone.

"I heard her coming," Allen barked dismissively while turning to greet Sara.

Dressed in black jeans, black sweater, and black running shoes, Allen Bauerman, at 5'9" in height, stood resolutely before Sara, extending his hand in a formal greeting.

"Pleasure to meet you, Miss Davis." He surveyed her with a stare.

"Sara, please," Sara replied, pulling her shoulders back with confidence.

"Very well. Where should we begin, *Sara?*" Allen emphasized, as he motioned toward the seating area in the corner of the cavernous space. Sara brushed her hair behind her ear as she made her way toward the minimalistic seating arrangement.

"Tell me what you plan to accomplish in the next two to three years, Allen," Sara began, as she carefully sat in the surprisingly uncomfortable chair. Based on the stiff leather, Sara was fairly confident that she was the first to be invited to sit there. Quickly scanning the room, it was apparent that the casual seating area had been recently added to the space. Sliding through the doorway, the assistant delivered both coffee and water to the table separating Allen from Sara, while keeping her eyes glued to the floor.

"I appreciate you getting right to the point, Sara. It is simple. I want to take this company public and dominate the social media software space," Allen said with a well-rehearsed confidence.

"Excellent, Allen. I appreciate your candid answer," Sara replied. "Help me with one detail." Sara paused for effect. "Why?" Sara asked, as she deliberately looked into Allen's eyes to analyze more than the words about to come from his mouth.

Allen's eyes narrowed as he contemplated the question. "Why?" He began with a slight strain in his voice. "Because that's what entrepreneurs do. They dominate their respective spaces. They win."

Sara sat quietly to allow Allen time to complete his response before she spoke again. "So, your purpose is to win?" she asked, while maintaining eye contact.

"Why wouldn't it be to win?" Allen quickly replied, growing increasingly impatient.

Sara was deliberate in her slow response. "I never said it wouldn't be your purpose. I'm just seeking to better understand your position. Define *win* for me."

Allen shifted his weight in the chair as he prepared his response. In the dead air moment, Sara produced a black leather journal and a black Mont Blanc pen from her handbag and started taking notes. The words began to form in Allen's head as he broke the silence.

"We win when we grow our revenue and maximize our profit. We do that by selling ads and data and outperforming our competition," he began. "Everyone wins when our shareholders realize a tremendous return on their investments." Leaning forward in his chair to retrieve his water, he looked at Sara with condescension. "Isn't that obvious, Miss Davis?"

Sara's eyes glanced above the top rims of her tortoise shell round glasses to catch the expression on Allen's face. She removed her glasses, placed her pen in the fold of her journal, and lifted her chin. "What is obvious to you is not always obvious to everyone around you. When the purpose of an organization is not clear, confusion frequently dominates the message both internally and externally. My role is to maximize clarity. People invest in clarity. And that, I believe, is the prime reason I am here." She replaced her glasses, freed the pen from her journal, and scrawled a few notes.

Allen nodded in consternation as he took his first drink of water. "Well, that could explain why I am constantly reminding my team what to do," Allen said with a hint of resignation in his voice.

"Tell me more about that," Sara said as she scribbled.

"I am constantly micromanaging everyone around here. I hire bright people on paper, but it seems they become idiots the moment they sit in the cubicle. It is very frustrating to be honest. Hell, if it wasn't for all the over-educated idiots, this place would be amazing," Allen waved both hands in disgust.

Sara's eyebrows began to slowly lift as Allen continued to speak. With more than 3,000 employees nationwide-half of them in Dallas-Bauerman was a highly sought-after employer. Yet, his employee turnover rates continued to climb as Allen's online employer ratings continued to drop. Sara made several notes in her journal as she practiced empathic listening, identifying key words Allen repeated as he described his organization. Sara jotted down the words *bright, idiots, frustrating.* What Sara was *not* hearing from the leader indicated that he had a blind spot. He was the true catalyst of the issue. Sara didn't hear him claim any responsibility for the overall ethos of the company.

Sara carefully wrote a note in her journal: *Where there is no vision, the people will perish.* Clara had repeated this to Sara on numerous occasions while working on issues in Congress. Clara would often remind the team, "We have to be clear why we are doing what we are doing so people don't miss what we believe to be obvious. We can never assume everyone knows what we know at the level we know it."

From the back of her journal, Sara produced a folded piece of paper. "I printed this off your website this morning." Sara unfolded the paper and placed it on the table. Allen reached to retrieve the paper and study its contents. "This states that your purpose is to connect people in community to create a better world," Sara added as Allen continued to study the page. Lowering the paper to his lap, Allen viewed Sara with puzzled bemusement.

"Ok. So, what's the point?" He said with a hint of disdain.

Sara looked down at her notebook. "You indicated earlier that your purpose was to win. Then you defined winning as growing revenue and profit through the sales of ads and data. Did I get that right?" she said as she flipped the page in her journal to check her notes.

"Yes, that is what I said," Allen replied.

"Then could you agree that it creates confusion when you publish one purpose externally, yet articulate a different purpose internally?" Sara asked with the confidence of a trial lawyer during closing remarks.

Allen studied Sara as he processed her words. It was rare that someone would answer him with blunt objectivity, without intimidation at his incredible intellect. "So, what are you saying?" he finally asked.

"Allen, you have two options when it comes to leading your employees. You can apply your positional power, something we refer to as forced-authority, or you can lead through authentic influence. Influence wielded as a result of your position and authority doesn't have the sustainable force required to create long-term results. Your influence needs to be seen as authentic and consistent," Sara explained.

"Authentic?" Allen repeated in a perplexed tone.

"This is a bigger conversation than today allows," Sara responded. "For now, I will leave you with this homework.

Authentic influence begins with a clear purpose. Currently, you have two stated purposes: one stated formally and the other informally. This has generated confusion, amongst other challenges. First, you need to be able to clearly and succinctly answer why you are here." Sara was undaunted.

"Aren't you confusing marketing jargon with the big picture?" Allen shot back.

Keeping her voice steady, Sara replied, "While you may be able to convince the public you have their best interest in mind for the time being, you will continue to struggle internally until you operate with a unified purpose. Case in point, I interviewed a recent recruit and they indicated that you helped close the deal to hire them by quoting the website purpose. The recruit indicated they wanted to work for an organization that was making a difference. Yet, their experience as an employee has been a complete deviation from your stated purpose."

Allen shot to his feet as the words washed over him like an acid bath. "Who told you that?!" he shouted as he turned to stare out the window overlooking the sea of employees below.

"Why do you ask?" Sara responded calmly.

"Because that type of disloyalty is not tolerated here. When I find out who told you that, that person is gone," Allen threatened, completely devoid of self-control.

"Allen, let's be clear. Any negative action against anyone my team interviews will result in immediate termination of our engagement." Sara deliberately applied the tone she learned from watching Clara deal with her peers in Congress.

Allen slowly turned around and exhaled the remaining breath in his lungs, forcefully adjusting to a more reasonable posture. For the first time in his career, someone–a woman no less–was willing to remain grounded in her convictions.

"Very well," were the only words to escape Allen's lips as Sara stood to gather her bag. Resolutely, she extended her hand.

"I will connect with you in one week to discuss your answers to your homework."

With a firm handshake, Sara turned to show herself out.

The
DEBRIEF

Sara dropped her bag onto the passenger seat of her Range Rover. Extending her arms onto the steering wheel and pressing her body deeply into the back of her seat, she let out a primal scream. Once she expelled all the air in her lungs at a decibel level that could shatter windows, the tension in her arms relaxed and she began to quietly weep. Soft sobs of frustration finally subsided, and Sara collected her thoughts before starting the Range Rover. Checking the mirror to correct any mascara mishaps, she took in a long cleansing breath, shifted into drive and drove back to the office.

A quick detour up McKinney Avenue brought Sara to a 100-year-old house tucked away on the side street of Routh Avenue. Once she found a place to park on the street, she made her way to the Crooked Tree Coffee House. Bypassing several coffee chains, she chose this independently owned coffee drinkers' nirvana, which had been converted from the old house. Sara relaxed in the bohemian vibe of the local roasting company and ordered a tall drip with one Splenda. Sinking into one of the funky mismatched chairs, Sara retrieved her phone to check her messages. On top of the list was a note from Kyle inquiring about the Bauerman meeting. After typing out a quick reply, Sara took one more lingering sip, gathered her bag and made her way back to the office.

Sara's corner office perfectly framed the expanding backdrop of the Dallas skyline. With floor-to-ceiling glass wrapping around two sides of the space, Sara was able to observe the activity below from anywhere in her office. On one wall, a 72" flat screen monitor was mounted, allowing for easy viewing of presentations and video conference calls. While seated at the conference room table directly in front of the massive monitor, Sara dialed Kyle's number.

His frame filled the screen, making Kyle appear larger than life while sitting comfortably in his office in New York City.

"Hmm," Kyle began as the picture came into perfect focus. "I can see you holding your Crooked Tree Coffee. Given it's almost noon, is this an indication of how your morning went? I do recall that mid-day coffee is your version of stress relief."

Sara smiled, enjoying the last sip of her drink. "How do you know that about me?"

"Listening to others often happens when people aren't speaking. A substantial part of what we do involves observation. We can learn as much, if not more, by paying close attention to what people are not saying, but doing," Kyle smiled kindly. "In all the years we've know each other, I noticed you would consistently drink coffee later than normal during stressful moments."

Sara shook her head in amazement at the finely-honed craft Kyle had developed by means of observation. His words prompted her to reflect differently on her meeting with Allen.

"So, what was the high/low of your meeting with Allen?" Kyle kept the conversation moving. Sara opened her leather journal to review her notes as she processed the last several hours.

"Allen has great potential," she uttered with a hesitant voice.

"You mean, he is a brilliant jerk?" Kyle replied with a wry grin, noting Sara's startled affirmation. "Allen is not the first client we have worked with whose entire worldview revolves around himself," Kyle reassured her.

Sara flipped the pages in her journal, struggling to come up with something positive to say about the meeting. Her silence spoke loudly as she wrestled to formulate the correct words in her mind.

"How did you feel once you left Allen's place?" Kyle inquired in a calming tone.

"Well, honestly, I cried," Sara's voice trailed off.

"I am sorry, Sara. Tell me about it."

Sara relaxed once she recognized his thoughtful compassion.

"After years of watching Clara deal with some of the harshest bullies in D.C., I thought I would be tougher actually. After today, I think I had completely underestimated her and how strong she really was," Sara began.

Kyle leaned forward in earnest expression. "Sara, I remember the first time Clara and I had this very conversation. She had just finished debating her opponent during her first run for office. Her strength was noteworthy throughout the debate. She was undaunted and unflappable. Yet, as soon as she stepped off the stage, she burst into tears."

Sara straightened in her chair as Kyle told the story, picturing the steel encased wall she had wrapped around her emotions during her meeting with Allen.

"It was that moment of vulnerability that set Clara's course going forward," Kyle offered as he continued to lean into the camera.

"What do you mean?" Sara pressed for more specific details.

"Clara and I both realized that having the right people in your life allows that level of vulnerability to be expressed. Vulnerability is important for every leader, but the expression of vulnerability must be appropriate for the audience." Kyle leaned back in his chair as he finished his last point.

Sara was busy jotting notes in her journal as Kyle was talking. *Situational vulnerability.* She recorded these two words and underlined them multiple times.

"Sara, it's important that you select your own personal board of directors for times such as these. Clara single-handedly filled that roll in your life for years, and now you are experiencing a significant void. I will always be there to counsel you, but given our working relationship, you will want someone else to share meaningful conversations with when you need to be your most vulnerable."

Sara slowly nodded in agreement, immediately recognizing that vapid space in her life left unattended without Clara.

"Now, what other insight did you gain from your time with Allen, aside from the fact that he is a brilliant jerk?" Kyle lightened the mood with a little sarcasm.

Sara's shoulders softened as she placed her arms on the conference room table and leaned toward the monitor. "Allen has a blind spot–a bit of victim mentality actually. He believes everyone in the room, except him of course, is the problem."

Kyle nodded, reflecting on the number of clients he had worked with who were plagued with the same diagnosis.

"Continue," Kyle said, unphased.

"His purpose is either not clearly stated or stated in various conflicting mediums. This has created enormous confusion within the organization. And, did I mention, he is a mild narcissist with disdain for women?" Her voice became stronger and more confident with each word.

Kyle paused appreciatively at Sara's debrief. "If I didn't know any better, I would swear you are describing Carson the first time you met him."

Sara startled and stared directly into the camera without blinking before she spoke. "You're right," she admitted, cupping her chin in her palm while gazing reflectively beyond the camera.

"And that relationship seemed to work out pretty well, wouldn't you agree?" Kyle chided.

Sara collapsed back into her chair, both perplexed and resigned.

"Isn't that different?" Sara responded with a hint of self-defense.

"Only difference is the fact that you are not going to marry Allen Bauerman. Unless I missed something?" Kyle smiled. Sara shot back a playful glare. "If I recall correctly, it was Clara who said, 'Even Carson Stewart deserves a second chance,'" Kyle gently offered.

Sara sat motionless, clearly recalling that statement that was made as Clara was exiting the car at Reagan Airport.

"You're right, Kyle." Sara took a shaky, centering breath. "So how do you suggest we proceed?"

"How did your meeting with Allen end?" Kyle asked. "Let's start at the ending."

"I gave him some homework. I instructed him to clearly articulate his actual purpose so we can rebuild the story internally and externally if necessary," Sara explained.

"Excellent! That is absolutely the right place for you to begin. Sara, I want to share how impressed I am with your patience," Kyle continued. "You demonstrated this same level of patience with Monica, and now I am witnessing your ability to apply this in a different situation with Allen. Most people rush to dictate an end solution, but you are taking your time to allow each person the opportunity to mentally and emotionally sort out their self-driven next step. When clients take the time to struggle with their own goals and expectations, their level of ownership over those intentions amplifies," Kyle coached.

"So, a vital part of our role is to continue to pose the right questions, allowing clients the opportunity to self-guide?" Sara paused and looked up from her notebook.

"Yes. To a degree," Kyle answered. "We should also be aware of danger zones when clients' ideas, regardless of the level of ownership, may potentially lead to more challenges." He spoke very deliberately. "So, for your next step, consider a potential response and prepare some of your follow-up questions to keep him moving in the right direction. If you need a backboard to bounce your questions off of, give me a ring." Kyle smiled once again to ensure Sara was confident in his sincerity.

"Thanks, Kyle. You don't know how much I appreciate your insight—especially after this morning."

Sara gently closed her journal. Kyle nodded, said goodbye and reached to turn off the monitor. Sara sat motionless in her chair as she contemplated the guidance Kyle had offered. His coaching was effortless, yet impactful—just what she needed to remain centered and emotionally in check. She knew she had only just scratched the surface layer of Kyle's bedrock of wisdom. One item stood out, however. Clara did leave an enormous, personal void when it came to vulnerability, and Sara knew it was time to find a personal board of directors to replace her dear friend.

The
BOARD

Sara grabbed her iPad and headed for the elevator bank in full stride. She tapped the down button multiple times to compensate for her stress as she gripped the iPad even tighter in her left hand. When the doors finally opened, she sighed, realizing she had the granite- and wood-clad compartment to herself. Facing forward, the doors slid shut, revealing the reflection of Sara from head to toe. Staring with great intensity into the mirrored doors, Sara's mind raced with ideas following her call with Kyle. She knew the only way to make sense out of the torrent of thoughts crashing through her mind was to spend time with the one person who understood her: Clara.

Once at street level, Sara made her way to Klyde Warren Park, the inner-city oasis constructed over a six-lane highway running through the heart of downtown Dallas. Finding a bench along the red crushed granite path, Sara settled in and opened her iPad. Scrolling through the files, she came to the next video on the list. Applying gentle pressure to the screen, Sara leaned back as the image of Clara appeared.

"Sweetie, you will remember this day. We worked late into the night on the CR while trying to juggle the interview with Carson. I think we both just consumed our body weight in Coke and pizza." Clara's words invoked an involuntary smile from Sara. "It is days such as today-19 hours of being "on"-when I appreciate our relationship the most."

Sara lowered the iPad onto her lap as she replayed that memorable day in her mind. "Clara must have recorded this message after 2:30 in the morning, shortly after I had collapsed into bed," Sara whispered to herself as the memories washed over her body like a warm bath.

The calendar that day was as complicated as one could be, even for a U.S. Congresswoman. Yet Sara remembered Clara remaining focused and attentive to each person in her presence. By midnight, the bulk of the work was done. Exhausted, the two of them sat down in her office to recap the day. For the next couple of hours, Clara shared intimate conversation with Sara.

Sara grinned uncontrollably as she recalled the conversation. Clara, as was her common practice, asked Sara to share her thoughts on specific moments of the day to review her perspective on what she experienced. In retrospect, Sara understood it was Clara's carefully employed method of teaching. Clara would ask, "What did you see that went well?" followed up by, "In your opinion, what would make it better next time?" Nodding imperceptibly, Sara recognized the cadence to Clara's inquires.

Lifting the tablet, Sara resumed the video.

"Regardless of how tired I think I am, when we sit to chat and reflect on what we have accomplished throughout the day, I am energized. While it is important to take time to reflect, sharing those moments with someone is vital to maintain your mental, emotional, and physical health. Selfishly, I've been consuming all of your time and filling that role in your life. Sooner rather than later, you will need to develop these relationships for yourself. You should consider selecting three people to fill this role. First, I would look for someone who has the miles and scars. You need this person for the collective wisdom of having 'been there and done that.' Second, you will need someone relatable, someone who is well tuned to your season of life. And finally, you should identify the person that is both a mentor and a mentee. Feedback from those you are influencing is also essential. Sara, sweetie, you have played that third role for me. I am eternally grateful for all I've learned from you over the years. You are a true blessing." Clara paused, her clear, unblinking eyes locking with the camera. After a long pause, she smiled, gave a wink and was gone.

Sara sat motionless for a brief moment as she absorbed Clara's words. She replayed those memorable moments multiple times in her mind as she stared at the blank screen on the tablet she was gripping. Kyle's timely counsel for gathering a personal board of directors and Clara's advice about selecting key people in her life to help maintain a healthy balance was not happenstance.

Pulling out her phone, Sara tapped a message to Abigail, "Hope your day is going well. Ring me when you get a break. Want to bounce something off you."

Scrolling through her calendar, she quickly searched for her next scheduled trip to New York. Sara had a board to select and the key members she had in mind were all there.

"Next week. Perfect," she said out loud for only the park squirrels to hear.

Springing from her seat, Sara took the extended route back to the office, meandering her way along the gentle, tree-lined path. So many important moments were transpiring. Carson's name was at the top of her favorites list on her phone. Tapping his contact information, she called the one person in her life who could identify the common thread weaving through all the changes.

****

Sara stepped onto 57th Street and headed toward 5th Avenue. The steady hum of traffic was only interrupted by the intermittent symphony of horns. Her brisk walk kept time with the steady beat of the city as she approached her rendezvous spot with Abigail.

Entering the thick brass door, she stepped into a world of wood paneled walls, caramel-colored leather seating and plaid-patterned accessories–the iconic and telltale accouterments of Ralph Lauren's *Polo Bar*. Walking the length of the bar, Sara spotted Abigail perched upon a round leather stool. Cradling a long-stemmed martini glass filled with a Vesper Martini in one hand, Abigail extended the other as Sara approached. With both drinks balanced in her hands, Sara and Abigail wrapped their arms around each other in a warm embrace.

"Wonderful to see you, Sara," Abigail said as she handed Sara the martini.

"And you, my friend," Sara smiled and pulled up a stool while enjoying the first sip of her drink. Settling in, she surveyed Abigail with a smile. "There is something I want to ask you." Sara leaned in closer to shield the revelry around them. "I have been considering some advice that has been recently provided by trusted mentors. It's time I put together a personal board of directors to support me as I embark upon a new direction in my life. I have thoughtfully considered three people who could make a meaningful and lasting impact upon my journey. You immediately came to mind as a vital member of that effort. It would be an honor to have you as part of my team." Sara placed her drink on the copper top bar, shifting on her stool to face Abigail.

Abigail had paused mid-drink to fully absorb the gravity of the request from Sara. Her eyes registered growing excitement at the prospect. She lowered her drink to fully meet Sara's gaze.

"I'd be honored." Abigail then reached out to grab Sara's hand. "Thank you for putting your faith in me."

Sara's smile radiated from deep inside her and warmed the room.

"The honor is all mine. By accepting my request, you are demonstrating your faith in me as well. And this is not a life sentence. I'm asking that each board member commit to a one-year term with the option of one additional year," Sara explained as she read Abigail's face.

"Brilliant!" Abigail exclaimed. "When are you planning the board meetings?"

"They will be informally scheduled, but I would hope to connect with you on a regular basis to check in," Sara outlined. "Abigail, I want you to hold me accountable for my outcomes and provide insight as I work through the next year in my role." Sara's face was flushed, partly from the martini, but mostly from the joy she was experiencing watching Abigail's story thread more tightly with hers.

Abigail extended her glass to propose a toast. Smiling mischievously, she sealed the occasion with a hearty jingle.

"May your years be blessed with more smiles than tears, and to you and yours, a hearty cheers!" The two glasses met, creating a perfectly pitched note to punctuate the moment.

Abigail leaned in and smiled.

"It is my great honor to serve on your board. Can you disclose who will be joining me?" Abigail took a long deliberate sip, purposefully navigating the bright spiral lemon peel.

"You are the first person I asked. From here, I am heading to see Joe. I'm counting on him to serve as my board chairman," Sara announced with a hint of pride in her voice.

"And the third?"

Sara's grin was uncontrollable as she responded, "There is a young veteran working at Joe's who has an amazing story. I really believe she would have a great deal to teach me if she will agree to serve in this manner."

"Did you say, *she*?" Abigail's eyes registered surprise.

"Yes, a real war hero who has withstood and conquered battles we could only read about," Sara explained with an authentic sense of pride.

"Sounds like someone I would enjoy meeting. Could be another book in the making for Carson." Abigail took a thoughtful sip of her martini and gave Sara a sly wink.

****

Joe's Place was quiet for this time of week. His regulars filled most of the stools around the bar, with the two exceptions at the far end. Any person who frequented Joe's knew those two stools were indefinitely reserved for Carson and Sara.

Making her way to the far end of the bar, Sara pulled out the ancient barstool and climbed into the well-worn seat as Joe appeared.

"And to what do I owe this great honor, my fair Sara?" Joe teased. Sara's face warmed at the sound of Joe's voice. "I know Carson is on the road, so this must mean you came just to see me." He placed both hands on the bar as he anticipated her drink order. With the precision of a well-honed purveyor of libations, Joe reached into the cooler to produce an ice-cold sparkling water. Retrieving a frosted mug, Joe carefully tilted the glass to match the angle of the bottle. In an effortless motion, he placed the cold drink directly before Sara.

"Based on what I see, this is also why you came in."

Sara cradled the cold drink in her hands. "Thank you," she smiled gratefully. "And you are right, I came in for more than one reason." Sara paused and held Joe's gaze hostage, her eyes conveying the gravity of the moment. "I have reviewed most of Clara's recorded messages to me, and her most recent advice is proving to be the most impactful so far," Sara continued. "That's really why I am here. I am forming a personal board of directors to guide and direct my journey, and I want you to be the head of my team."

Joe stood motionless, unable to look away from Sara's sincere and soul-baring request. With both arms extended against the bar for support, his thick black beard concealed much of what he was thinking. As he gripped the bar, his mind ascended and descended on the emotional rollercoaster that first brought this young woman back into his life. A combination of gain and loss, both heartwarming and heartbreaking, he recognized the depth of what her request actually *offered* him. After a brief moment, a slow and trembling grin appeared from behind his thick hairy shield.

"I'm in, kid. What do I need to do?" Joe's brevity protected the floodgates pressing against his chest.

"Not much more than what you are already doing," Sara smiled, relieved, yet not surprised by his acceptance. "I just need to formalize it…plus," Sara paused before she finished her sentence.

"Plus, what?" Joe's expression was quizzical, grateful for a distraction.

"I need a favor," Sara asked with a hint of hesitation.

"Name it," Joe responded firmly, his emotions tempered by her potential "to do" list.

"I am asking three people to join my board," Sara explained. "I would like those three people to be you, Abigail, and Patterson." Sara counted each one on her fingers.

Joe remained unblinking. "What's the favor?"

"Will you help me approach her?" Sara asked, nodding in the direction of Patterson. Joe looked over Sara's shoulder to spot Patterson in the far corner of the bar cleaning tables.

Wasting no time, Joe bellowed across the sparsely crowded bar, "Patterson!"

Hearing Joe's voice, Patterson spun around to make eye contact with him. Joe motioned for her with a subtle nod of his head, indicating she should make her way to the bar.

"Sara has something she wants to ask you that I think is worth considering," Joe began as Patterson wiped her hands on the well-worn apron tied around her waist.

Sara darted a curious look at Joe and softly whispered, "That's how you help?" Joe shrugged his shoulders, revealing a sheepish smile.

"Yes, ma'am?" Patterson inquired, nervously shifting between her feet.

"I am putting together a personal board of directors," Sara smiled warmly. "They will be a group of people who can help me remain accountable to my outcomes while allowing me to lean on them for advice and counsel." Patterson's eyes widened slightly as she listened to Sara. "I would very much like to have you join my board, Patterson. You are the missing link that will complete this effort and offer great value to me."

Patterson glanced at Joe for a hint at what to do next. The last time she had offered to serve someone else, it had ended very painfully and dramatically altered her own life course.

"You should do this," Joe assured her in an encouraging tone.

"Not sure I know what to do, ma'am," Patterson replied nervously.

Sara noted her shaking hands and understood her trepidation. "Please consider it, Patterson. It only requires you to spend some informal time with me throughout the year, and at the end of the year, we determine if we want to extend it for another twelve months." Sara's tone was reassuring yet firm.

"I know very little about your business," Patterson mumbled while subtly dropping her head, her insecurity still apparent.

"That is quite alright," Sara continued her reassurance. "I already have business experience on the board. You bring a unique and important insight to the team."

The sparkle in Sara's eyes ignited a ray of hope in Patterson. She lifted her head to meet Sara's gaze.

"Your view on how a team works with purpose is second to none. I truly look forward to learning things from you that no one else can offer."

Sara's authentic passion ignited Patterson's feeble confidence. Patterson stood taller as she smiled at Joe then slowly turned to Sara.

In a surprise move, clearly startling Patterson, Sara reached forward and enclosed Patterson with a bone-crushing hug. Squeezing her tightly, Sara softly whispered, "Thank you," as a single tear cascaded down Patterson's rosy cheek.

The
STORY

Monica stepped into her office to find Sara waiting in the plush seating area. The Portman New York City office faced Madison Avenue and consumed three floors of the towering glass clad structure in the center of Mid-Town. The office was designed appropriately for the City with only a hint of Monica's Texas roots attached to the wall behind her desk. She had displayed two folded flags: one of Old Glory and the other of the state flag of Texas, as a subtle reminder of her home soil. Both flags had been presented to Monica's father from the troops in Fort Hood, Texas, commemorating Martin Portman's humble support and service.

Sara rose to her feet to greet her friend.

"I do hope you haven't been waiting long," Monica began as the two embraced.

"Just long enough to admire your view and the numerous awards covering the walls," Sara said as her eyes scanned the room to acknowledge the mementos.

"My staff gets a bit carried away at times, hanging pictures and plaques on much of the free space. It does, however, still serve as a humble reminder of why we do what we do," Monica said as she motioned for Sara to make herself comfortable.

"Perfect segue for why I am here," Sara said with a smile. "The last time we were together, I challenged you with some homework."

"I remember," Monica nodded in thoughtful agreement. "I have been giving it a fair amount of consideration, to say the least."

"And?" Sara prodded.

Monica made her way to the hidden fridge in the corner of the office. Opening the simple wood clad door, she produced two mini bottles of Coke. Turning dramatically with the contents of her hands visible to Sara, she said, "Interest you in a morning indulgence?"

"Yes! Don't mind if I do." Sara reached for the carbonated beverage, some liquid joy to accompany the morning. Taking the bottle from Monica, the two tapped the glass necks together, finding camaraderie in the ice-cold delight.

"The two questions you asked me were more of a challenge than I anticipated. Contemplating a story being told about me sent my mind into a place of near terror." Monica paced the floor, holding the bottle with both hands.

"Terror?" Sara was surprised. "Tell me more."

Monica paused and took another sip. "My first thought was about people talking behind my back, calling me a trust fund baby and judging me as undeserving of the CEO spot. I really let that fictitious committee of voices get into my head."

Sara remained silent, studying Monica as she continued to unpack her thoughts.

"I began second guessing everything; that is, until I actually took the time to ask someone about it." She turned with a crooked smile.

"What did you learn?" Sara asked gently, a subtle prod to maintain the flow of thought.

"I learned that people will tell you the truth if you have taken the time to build authentic relationships with them." Monica paused in satisfaction. She finished the last drink of her Coke and placed the bottle on the small conference table in her office.

"And when you asked, what did you discover?" Sara continued to gently prod.

"I discovered that the story actually being told about me is encouraging and deeply humbling," she said with a tone of true humility. "People believe I know our business and am both well-qualified and willing to learn. This combination, I am discovering, is important for any leader. Most profound, they see my strength and compare me to my father." Monica paused, those last words triggering an uncontrollable impulse to succumb to the thick moisture gathering behind her eyes.

Sara reached out to rest her hand on Monica's shoulder. "Your dad is very proud of you." Sara's reassuring tone instilled a hushed reverence. Monica nodded gratefully, patting Sara's hand.

"The real test was authentically answering your second question: *What is the story I want told beyond my resume?*" Monica paused. "Sara, I have to admit, until you asked me to think about it, I viewed my life and my resume as a symbiotic relationship."

Sara smiled and reclined in the overstuffed coach.

"What did you learn from the experience?" Sara asked.

"That my life is much bigger than my resume." Monica regained vigor in her voice.

"So, what I hear you saying is you want your legacy to be the work you are doing at the company *plus* something more?" Sara qualified.

"Yes! That *is* it, Sara. I am very proud of the work we are accomplishing at the company, but there is also more inside of me beyond this company."

"How does *that* story read?" Sara asked, to encourage Monica's vibrant thought process.

"The story I want to write beyond my resume is making a difference in the lives of people around the country and beyond. It is a story about not backing down from the big issues outside the walls of a corporate fortress. Win or lose, I want a legacy of remaining in the fight, giving a voice to the people beyond my corporate walls," Monica spoke with full-throated conviction as she gazed over the mass of humanity teeming in the City below.

Sara stood to join Monica as the two surveyed the City. "What do you need to change to ensure that this story is the one told about you someday?" Sara asked in a calm yet deliberate tone.

"I've given this some serious thought, and after speaking with dad, I've decided to run for office," Monica said without breaking her stare out the expansive window. "That endeavor is where I could use your counsel, Sara."

Sara thought for a moment before speaking, "I completely agree, Monica. Your purpose is much bigger than the company," Sara began. "I can also picture your story taking you to D.C., making a difference globally." Her reassuring tone reflected the wisdom of someone with deep knowledge of the workings inside the Beltway. "And I know just the seat you should represent," Sara added, eyes crinkling as a smile spread from ear to ear.

"If you had told me I needed to run for office when we first met, my response would have been to question your sanity. But pressing me to consider my story beyond my resume brought me to this conclusion on my own. Thank you for that gift of patience and understanding, Sara." Monica smiled back with a deep gratitude.

"Truly my pleasure, old friend. Now, we have some work to do over the next year to get you ready for a viable campaign. I want to make certain the people trust that your heart has been always shaped to serve others. Wearing that heart on your sleeve as a Lawmaker is a story that will definitely look good on you." Sara gave Monica a warm embrace before collecting her bag. After more words of affirmation, Sara departed to share the good news with Kyle before catching her flight back to Dallas.

****

Sara knew a change of venue would be helpful for her next meeting with Allen Bauerman. The century old building on Lower Greenville provided the perfect neutral ground to continue their conversation. H&G Supply restaurant inhabited the rustic shotgun building with exposed brick walls and old painted concrete floors. The menu consisted of clean, wholesome food, both tasty and nutritious.

The lunch meeting was confirmed for 11:30 to beat the rush in that popular Dallas eatery. Sara arrived on time and was able to command a prime table for lunch. Ordering a cold *Topo Chico* with lime, she closed the menu, having ordered many times before. Checking her messages to ensure Allen had not texted her to alert her to any unexpected tardiness, she discovered a message from Abigail.

"You are mentally and emotionally prepared to handle this today. Stay focused and on point as we discussed. Call me after if you have time." Gently pressing on the message revealed the row of emoticons. Tapping the heart, Sara let Abigail know her appreciation for the words of encouragement.

The low hum of the restaurant slowly increased in volume as the hip bistro began to fill to capacity. Glancing at her watch, Sara decided to send a quick text to Allen's assistant inquiring about his whereabouts. The reply was disheartening, but not unexpected.

"It's my fault. He just left five minutes ago to head your way. I am very sorry for the delay. Please forgive me."
"Not to worry. Thank you for trying."

Sara exhaled a sigh of frustration as she pushed send, recognizing the subtle cover job by Allen's assistant. Realizing she had several minutes still to wait, Sara signaled to her server and ordered another cold drink. The additional time allowed Sara to send a quick message to Kyle to provide an update.

"It seems our client doesn't value my time. Has me waiting over 40 minutes with no apparent emergency or conflicting meeting, according to his EA," Sara quickly tapped with both thumbs.

The response from Kyle was much quicker than Sara anticipated. "Unacceptable for any client to be deliberately disrespectful of OUR time," Kyle replied. "Let me know if I can help, but do not hesitate to fire the client should you feel it is not the right fit going forward. At times, you have to be willing to walk away in order to make the biggest impact going forward."

Sara exhaled a more relaxed sigh after reading Kyle's message, gratefully acknowledging the value of true support.

"Thank you, Kyle," Sara texted in response as she contemplated how to handle Allen if and when he showed up. As the text cleared her phone, Sara heard a voice bellow into the now crowded restaurant.

"Had an emergency at the office. Couldn't be avoided," were the first words out of Allen Bauerman's mouth as he pulled out the metal chair to take a seat. Sara was stunned at the relative ease in which Allen was willing to conveniently bend the truth for the situation. Reaching back into her memory, Sara recalled a conversation with Clara about situational integrity and how moments like these gradually corrupt a person's soul until their integrity is a mere apparition of times past.

Collecting her thoughts, Sara carefully chose her words. "The late Congresswoman Clara Becker once told me that the greatest asset we contribute to each day is our character. Would you agree, Mr. Bauerman?" her words hung weightily in the aromatic room. Allen slowly lowered his menu to make eye contact with Sara.

With a measured tempo he considered his response. "I would."

Sara maintained eye contact with Allen. "She would also remind each of her staff that the cornerstone of our character is our integrity. Would you also agree, Mr. Bauerman?" Sara caught his attention with the increasing intensity in her voice. Allen simply nodded in agreement as he clenched his jaw.

"You have published on your website and with posters in your office communicating integrity as one of your company values. So, a reasonable person would conclude that integrity should be important to you as the founder and leader of the company. Is that a fair statement, Mr. Bauerman?" Sara continued in the steady cadence of a skilled attorney during closing arguments.

Allen's clenched jaw exposed the flexing of the muscles in his face as he reluctantly nodded in response to Sara's line of questioning.

Taking a long drink of her cold water, Sara placed her glass gently on the table, leaning closer to pose the next penetrating question. "How would you *define* integrity, Allen?" Realizing that he had been masterfully backed into the corner, he had no choice but to quote the same words he dictated as the values of the company.

"Integrity is keeping our commitments and doing what we say we will do." His voice forced each word.

"Allen, you need to hear this feedback. The story being told about you is a confusing tale of mixed messages. On one hand you have created game-changing technology for the future of the tech space. The ability to enrich the lives of others, both literally and figuratively, is within your reach. On the other hand, any progress forward will forever be compromised when your words and deeds fail to align." Sara paused to allow the straight talk to resonate.

Allen was often the smartest person in the room and, unsurprisingly, the most domineering. His ability to work complex problems in his head was just one of the other-worldly traits from the young wunderkind. Today, sitting across the table from Sara Davis, he pushed his enormous intellect to the far reaches of his capacity. Granting Allen a reprieve, two servers placed individual bowls of steaming food before quickly exiting, which allowed Allen to take the time to further process Sara's insights.

"I want to apologize," were his first words, breaking through the background white noise from the full capacity restaurant. Sara allowed Allen to continue before she spoke. "My actions have been less than desirable," Allen ruminated, fork in hand, holding the next bite of food. He proceeded to eat, silently and dismissively, clearly not understanding and accepting Sara's well-placed wisdom.

Sara pulled her shoulders back and sat taller in her seat. Placing her fork on the table next to the bowl, she made direct eye contact with Allen with a caring, yet resolute gaze.

"Thank you for the apology, Allen," She began. "This will be our last meeting. Ellis International is ending our relationship with Bauerman today," she finished with a deliberately firm tone.

Allen's eyes registered shock as Sara's words shot across the table like a bullet aimed directly at his heart. Paralyzed, Allen was unable to speak or move, frozen in time and space by the direct hit. In a casual gesture, Sara motioned for the check, which signaled the pending end of the lunch meeting. For one of the few times in his life, Allen was out of his depth with no idea what to do. Unable to think on his feet and properly handle the situation before him, Allen resorted to the only tactic he knew.

"You can't quit. I'll sue you and Ellis International for breach of contract," Allen bellowed, face ablaze with a brewing inferno. Sara continued to sign the receipt for lunch, undaunted by Allen's words. Once she had signed her name, she calmly looked up to respond.

"That is certainly your right, Allen. Once you actually read the contract, however, you will find our unrestricted ability to sever our relationship at any time should we determine a client has an irreparable character," Sara stated, emphasizing the word *irreparable*.

"Irreparable?" Allen repeated in shock as Sara collected her bag and coat. "I know I've made some mistakes and can be a bit abrasive at times, but *irreparable*? That is absolutely ridiculous!" He shoved his chair away from the table.

Sara paused as she stood up to leave. Leaning over the table, she looked him directly in the eye.

"There is an old saying that there is no such thing as bad publicity. Maybe putting your character on trial will be good for business," she said as she walked toward the door. After two steps, Sara paused and turned toward Allen who was frozen with fury and humiliation. "Should you need an attorney to defend you, give me a call. I do believe you are worth defending. You can *repair* your story, Allen. But first, you must *repair* your character and only you can make that decision."

Before he could make recompose, she disappeared through the wood and glass door.

The
EVENT

"Please join us at the gathering of friends, family, and dignitaries as we recognize the longstanding philanthropic work of Clara Becker," read the invitation that was embossed in feathery gold lettering. The black-tie event was to be held in Washington at the Smithsonian Castle. Sara held the invitation gently in her hand as Carson sat silently at her side, allowing Sara to process the moment.

"I should go," Sara decided, looking up to meet his gaze. "Apparently, we have been given an entire table." She gave him a melancholy smile.

"From Kyle?" Carson read her conflicted emotions.

"It says the invite is from the office of Congressman Simon Sanders," Sara said as she stared at the hand-lettered card tipped in gold leaf.

"Well, who do you want to invite?" Carson asked, as he eased off the couch to create a Dagwood-style sandwich. Sara rested the invitation in her lap as she contemplated the question from Carson.

"Want a sandwich?" Carson asked as he pulled items from the refrigerator to build his creation. Sara turned to watch

Carson fumble with a pile of lunchmeat before she decided to join him in the kitchen.

"Watching you at work in the kitchen is a beautiful thing," Sara said with a radiating smile. Carson paused, knife in one hand and a jar of spread in the other hand. He returned the smile before licking the knife clean.

Sara shook her head while letting out a burst of laughter. "Don't you dare stick that knife back in the jar!" she exclaimed, reaching for the tainted instrument while simultaneously wrapping her arm around Carson's waist to give him a gentle hug. Resting her head on Carson's shoulder she sighed, "This event sounds like a great opportunity for a board meeting."

Carson stopped mid-motion as he was lifting the two-fisted sandwich to his month.

"Board meeting?"

"Yep, board meeting." Sara took control of Carson's hands, directing them to her mouth, as she devoured a sizable portion of the multi-layered monstrosity.

****

The night of the event unfolded like a scene from a Disney storybook. The Castle was aglow as streams of black cars deposited the elite of D.C. to the main entrance of the 150-year-old red sandstone landmark. Upon entering the building, all the grandeur of the last century and a half, enveloped the attendees. The gothic architecture, in perfect harmony with dramatic lighting, intensified the drama of the entrance. The ambiance emanated from floor to ceiling, shadows enhancing the intricate details delicately carved into a series of arches overhead. The event was purposefully held at the quintessential setting for a D.C. power event.

Sara and Carson arrived and were joined by Kyle and Emily. Next to arrive was Abigail, dressed in a long, strapless, hourglass red dress. Sara greeted her warmly as she entered the majestic hall, placing a gentle kiss on her cheek in welcome.

"You look stunning this evening," Sara said to both Abigail and Emily, gazing with rapt admiration as the two stood in the soft glow of the lights. Carson subtly stepped in and pointed towards the door.

"Who is that with Joe and Marisa?"

Turning towards the entrance, Sara did a double take, uncertain if that was, in fact, Patterson walking towards her.

An imposing woman with long, black, wavy hair was stepping across the threshold. No ball cap in sight, her voluminous locks were pulled to one side in a subtle, yet stylish sweep. A deep navy blue, velour gown wrapped around her thin, toned body, accentuating every curve. Her face glowed with the right amount of blush while a little mascara framed her bright, ocean-blue eyes. The color of the dress accentuated flecks of deep navy and aquamarine shining from the depth of her gaze. She walked with grace and power, her entrance like the arrival of a striking sapphire dispelling the gothic shadows that framed her silhouette. As she stepped into the grand hall, every head turned to catch a glimpse of the beauty wrapped in blue.

Sara was frozen for a brief moment, incredulous that this woman was the same Patterson who wiped down the tables at Joe's.

"You are a vision to behold, my friend," Sara gushed as she leaned in to give her a gentle embrace. Patterson's face began to flush.

"Thank you, ma'am. Marisa is a miracle worker." Patterson nodded towards Marisa while holding onto Sara's hand, squeezing tightly to restrain her from going too far.

"No miracle needed. You are a natural beauty," Marisa stated and smiled as she stepped toward the two ladies. Sara reached over to kiss Marisa on the cheek.

"I am so very glad you are here. Thank you," Sara said softly for only Marisa to hear.

Making their way to table seven in the massive hall, the group claimed their seats. Once seated, Sara leaned across the table to speak to Kyle.

"Thank you for being here tonight. It means a great deal to me, Kyle."

"I wouldn't miss it for anything, Sara," Kyle responded just as Simon Sanders appeared tableside.

"So very glad each of you could join me this evening," Simon said, eyeing the attendees. The members at the table smiled warmly at their host for the evening; however, Patterson sat expressionless as she came face-to-face with Simon Sanders for the first time in years.

Once Simon appeared, Patterson dropped her head to avoid eye contact with the Congressman. Picking up on the odd move, Joe leaned over to Patterson to check in.

"Everything okay?" he said in a hushed tone.

"Fine, sir," she replied. "Didn't realize the Congressman was at our table."

Once Simon was settled into his seat at the table, the program began. Salads were first, followed by two quick speeches recognizing Clara's lifetime of serving. By the time the main course arrived at the table, the conversation had dwindled to an uncomfortable hush until Patterson finally spoke up.

"Congratulations on your win, Captain," her voice rose over the oversized flower arrangement that marked the center of the setting.

Simon froze. Leaning to his left to see around the flowers, Simon startled at the site of Master Sergeant, Bethany Patterson. Finishing off the remaining red wine in his glass, Simon regained his composure.

"Good to see you, Master Sargent."

What little conversation that was happening came to a complete stop. Every head motioned between Simon and Patterson as each of the members of the group worked to solve the mystery of their apparent familiarity. Sara, the first to make the connection, leaned forward to speak.

Looking at Simon but speaking to Patterson, Sara said, "Congressman Sanders was your Captain during your last deployment, is that correct?"

Patterson nodded gently without answering.

"If I recall correctly, it was his last deployment that garnered Congressman Sanders The Metal of Honor," Sara continued, locking eyes with Simon who was beginning to conspicuously loosen his tie.

The stunned silence at the table was broken by the next speaker who introduced a video of Clara being interviewed just before her death. As the lights dimmed, Simon took the opportunity to turn his chair from the glares of those seated around table seven.

On two large screens positioned at both ends of the hall, Clara's image filled the frames. The overwhelming site of their dear friend caught the group by surprise. Carson reached over to take Sara's hand and give it a reassuring squeeze. As soon as Clara began to speak, Carson realized the video was shot on the last day of interviews for the book. The room filled with the sound of Clara's Texas drawl.

> "At the end of it all, I am most proud of the people I have had the privilege to serve," Clara said into the camera. "The people of The Great State of Texas have honored me for more than two decades, allowing me to represent them here in our nation's capital." She paused as the interviewer in the video continued to ask her questions. "The secret to surviving Washington? After all these years I can say with all confidence that if your character is not worthy, you might make it to Washington, heck, you might even make it back to Washington a time or two, but you will never be truly effective without your character. It is no secret that the secret is contained in your character."

With those words the room erupted in uncontrollable applause.

The
VISIT

The crowd at Joe's place was the new normal-busy and about to get busier. Marisa was behind the bar with Joe and the team, sending burgers upstairs as quickly as they were made. No one noticed the man entering the bar with the black leather jacket and ball cap pulled down to fully conceal his eyes. Scanning the room for a table, the man selected the one yet to be cleaned-adjacent to a table that had recently been wiped down by Patterson.

Taking his seat with his back to the wall, the man carefully surveyed the crowded room as if he was in search of a lost treasure. Marisa's barback arrived at the man's table to take his order.

"What can I get ya?" the waiter's voice squeaked.

"Johnny Walker Blue," said the voice from behind the hat. "And I'll have a burger."

"Got it. Thanks. And I will get this table cleared off for you," the squeaky voice replied as he shuffled away, yelling downstairs to Patterson.

Marisa read the slip of paper handed to her with the drink order and paused. The last time she poured a Johnny Walker Blue was for a bachelor party. Scanning the room to see who would order the high-end drink, she noticed the man in the cap. Retrieving her phone from her hip pocket, she sent a quick note to Joe and asked him to come upstairs. Realizing how rare it was for Marisa to text during business hours, Joe appeared in a matter of seconds only to find Patterson holding her dish tub, frozen before the man in the hat.

Looking up from beneath the bill of his hat, the face of Congressman Simon Sanders was revealed.

"Hello, Patterson. Good to see you again," Simon began. "I am sorry we were unable to catch up more at the event last week. I must say you caught me off guard in your dress."

Patterson stood quietly before the table, her hands gripping her dish tub.

"What do you want, Captain?" Patterson said in a barely audible voice.

"Just wanted to see how you are getting along. War had been hell and not everyone made it out, even if they went home," Simon added.

Setting the glass of scotch on the table, Joe stood up straight to reveal the fullness of his perfectly toned body, still capable of breaking a person into pieces.

"Your drink, Congressman," Joe said in his scary voice, one he saved for the reluctant drunk who refused to act like a gentleman while in his establishment.

"Thank you. Joe, is it?" Simon offered his hand.

Joe reached for his ever-present white towel to wipe off his hands while ignoring Simon's extended hand.

"You have every right to be suspicious," Simon said while slowly withdrawing his extended limb. "I assure you, my intentions are noble."

His words elicited a deep sigh from Patterson. Simon lifted his arms to signal a type of surrender, while nodding his head in agreement with Patterson's assessment of her old Captain. Standing to his feet, Simon reached inside his pocket to produce a money clip of folded hundred-dollar bills. Pulling two from the stack, he let them drop on the table. Lifting the glass of scotch from the table, he threw back the drink, consuming its contents in one swift motion.

"Patterson, I wish you well." Simon paused for a brief moment before turning on his heel and making his way to the door.

As Simon neared the door, a voice darted across the room. "Why did you come, Captain?" Patterson moved a little closer to Joe.

Simon paused, his back still to Patterson. Turning slowly, he removed his cap, holding it in both hands as he nervously stared at the floor. He finally lifted his head.

"It was something Clara said in her video at the event," Simon began, nervously squeezing his hat. "Between seeing you and hearing her words, I've been overwhelmed with memories of our last tour. I've made regrettable choices along the way that have profited me greatly, but in the end, I have lost my soul." Simon paused, a single tear forming in his right eye. "You saved my life once. I guess by coming here, seeing you again, I thought I might find a way to save my life again."

Trying his best to collect himself, Simon replaced the black cap tightly upon his head and turned toward the door. With his hand on the old brass handle, Simon pulled the door open that stood between him and the City beyond.

"We are here to help, sir," a strong voice traveled across the room, beckoning him to turn one last time. Simon faced

Patterson, that tear threatening to close the distance between them.

"War is hell, sir. But with the right people around you, it is possible to make it back. It is possible to make it right."

Simon smiled with a look of surrender and relief, blinked in agreement and slipped out the door. Patterson and Joe stood motionless while watching Simon disappear into the streets of the City. Turning to clear the table where Simon had been sitting, Patterson slowly picked up the money Simon had left on the table, which revealed an object that caused Patterson to collapse into the chair. Joe turned to check on Patterson and found, sitting in front of her, the blue ribbon with 13 embroidered stars attached to the green laurel, surrounded by the five-pointed star of The Metal of Honor.

Joe looked at Patterson who was sobbing uncontrollably as years of emotional distress burst through her physical being. Placing his hand on her shoulder, Joe softly said, "Simon was who you saved that day."

Patterson continued to sob as she nodded her head in agreement.

"How did Simon take credit for the metal?" Joe asked as he slipped into the chair beside Patterson.

Gaining her composure, Patterson looked at Joe. "I carried him three miles to the landing zone, only to collapse when I arrived. Just before the heli landed, Simon came to, picked me up, and held me. He thought I was dead. The rescue team thought he was saving me so that was the story he let them tell. My injuries were so severe that, by the time I recovered, the story of his heroics were already long exposed to the public."

Joe sat stunned as he processed the story.

Through bloodshot eyes, Patterson looked at Joe and continued, "The more powerful Simon became, the stronger the message became for me to keep my mouth shut. That message never came from him directly, but over the years it became clear that if I said anything, I would regret ever coming home from the war.

Reaching over, Joe picked up the metal and placed it gently in Patterson's hands. He then placed one hand on her shoulder while holding her other hand in a firm grip.

Joe said, "This metal has finally found its way home."

Closing her eyes, Patterson breathed out a sigh of cleansing relief.

The
EPILOGUE

The smell of freshly roasted coffee beans filled the air of the tiny cafe in the heart of Dallas. Sara sunk into her favorite eclectic mid-century chair in the corner of what used to be the building's living room well over a century ago. Steam rose from the white porcelain cup of coffee that Sara had placed on the delicate wooden table next to her chair. Retrieving her iPad, Sara pulled it onto her lap and reached to take a deliberate sip of the hot Honduran mixture. She hesitated to turn on her iPad as she knew what awaited her. The last unwatched video from Clara would also be a final goodbye.

From her vantage point in the house, Sara eyed the other connoisseurs of local roasted coffee, mostly hidden behind their laptops or deeply engaged in their conversations. She let herself become distracted for a moment, ruminating on what had brought each patron to the coffee shop that day: the student buried deep in his thick books emblazed with the red stamp on the end pages identifying the local university; the two girls locked in giggles of friendship, catching up after an extended period of separation; two entrepreneurs working together on their upstart company goals for the new year. All of these present bodies were searching for wisdom, knowledge, and connection from a wide variety of sources. Sara's gaze finally rested on the young girl reading a book in the far corner, hair pulled into a messy ponytail. As the twenty-something took a drink of her coffee, she shifted her weight in the oddly shaped chair to reveal the cover of her morning read. *The Lawmaker* immediately caught Sara's eye.

Sara's heart swelled and for the first time in months, there was no rush of tears. At that profound moment, Sara registered the impact of Clara on the next generation of leaders. Her heart pulsed as a rush of blood filled the rest of her body with the satisfaction that all would be okay-that *she* would be okay-and that her friend, Clara Becker, The Lawmaker, would always be written onto the pages of her life. With those thoughts awash in her mind, Sara turned on her iPad to absorb the final words of wisdom recorded just for her.

"Good morning, sweetie," echoed the immediately recognizable Texas accent that filled Sara's mind with the essence of Clara Becker. "We finished the book yesterday. Carson has been outstanding. A true gift." Clara smiled. "Between the book and these videos, I have left you with all but one last bit of wisdom. We have talked a lot about character, and now I want to lead you gently down the path of character restoration. Repairing a scarred character requires work-a lot of work-but it is possible. Just look at Carson. The path to restoration begins in the engine of our influence, which is fueled by trust. Think of influence as a Venn diagram with three overlapping circles. In one circle you have to be you, the authentic you, not who you think someone wants you to be. The fakeness of trying to be someone else eventually comes out. In the next circle is compassion. To build sustainable influence, you must be empathic towards others in the way you serve and are generous. In the final circle is clarity. People may value integrity, but they follow clarity. You must be clear in how you communicate your thoughts and feeling. Remember back to your Communications 101 class in college? The old saying remains true. Tell 'em what you want to tell 'em, then tell 'em about it, then tell 'em what you just told told 'em. Essentially, the key is to be clear." Clara was waving her hands like a chief conductor of an orchestra finale as she made each point. "That's it, sweetie, everything we've talked about in some quick summary. Regardless of what you decide to do going forward, I want you to hide these visuals in your heart. They will serve you well as you continue to serve others on your journey. And always remember, the best is yet to come." Clara gave one last wink, the final note of her well-crafted symphony, and was gone.

The bell attached to the top of the roughly hewn door gave a muted chime as Kyle entered. The original wood floors, worn from years of traffic, gave an ancient creek as Kyle made his way to the makeshift counter to order.

"Cup of your house coffee, please," Kyle addressed the barista. The sound of coffee pouring into the diner-style white mug was a language of its own in the homey space.

Kyle walked the few steps into the long-forgotten living room, the walls and ceiling tilting slightly out of plumb from a century of settling soil. Pulling out the mismatched chair, Kyle set his hot beverage on the table and gently reclined in front of Sara.

"Love this place," he said, thoroughly enjoying his first sip. "Can't find this kind of atmosphere in New York."

"Nothing against the big chains," Sara began, "but there is just something about this place. I used to come here from time to time when I was in college to get away from campus and be alone." Sara was reflective on years past. "Thank you for coming down to see me," Sara said as she placed her iPad in her bag.

"Watching Clara?"

"The last video," Sara said as she ironically finished the last sip of her morning coffee.

"Learn anything?" Kyle was inquisitive. Sara smiled while nodding her head.

"It seems the last few months have been a flood of learning," she said with a hint of a chuckle in her voice. "For years, I was witness to Clara's wisdom first hand. It was only when I needed to put these truths into action for myself that her words really came to life. I've learned the real transformation begins when knowledge is put into action," Sara added.

"Is it a fair statement to say that, over the last several months, you have had a rich series of meaningful moments that resulted from your application of wisdom?" Kyle asked.

Sara smiled as she nodded in agreement with Kyle.

Kyle reached into the worn leather bag he faithfully carried with him everywhere, producing a black leather covered journal and a small box. Kyle placed the two items on the table.

"I've noticed your discipline in taking notes in a journal, a practice I admire," Kyle began. "So, I got you something for your journey. Transformational learning takes hold when you tell the story of your meaningful moments."

Sara picked up the small box first. Lifting the lid on the top of the long high gloss box revealed a black Mont Blanc fountain pen.

"I took the liberty of filling it and having the bottle of ink sent to your office. The leather journal had a simple inscription towards the bottom of the front cover: *Be in the Arena.*"

"Thank you, Kyle." Sara's expression registered the excitement of a Christmas morning.

"My pleasure," Kyle replied. "I wanted you to have a place to record the stories you are gathering. You will find, when the time is right, that these stories will help you shape the life of someone important to you. Just as Clara's stories have shaped you."

Sara softly caressed the front cover before she pulled it open to expose the inside cover and the inscription from Kyle: *Sara, may the words you record continue to shape your authentic influence as you dare greatly in the arena. Kyle.*

Sara took her time to reread the words of her new mentor before turning the page to reveal the first blank writing space.

"So, what has been learned over the last several months?" Kyle watched Sara retrieve the fountain pen from its holder. Quietly, Sara recorded her first note as Kyle looked on.

"Our ability to lead begins with our ability to influence others. Forced authority in not sustainable; authentic influence is," Sara said as she wrote on the page.

Kyle nodded gently.

"Agreed," Kyle said. "Where have you seen that play out recently?" Kyle asked as Sara finished writing. Looking up at Kyle, Sara processed the question quickly.

"Allen Bauerman," she replied.

"How so?" Kyle asked with a Socratic tone.

"Allen has chosen, as of now, to use his positional power to create a command and control environment within his company. Forced authority coupled with misaligned words and deeds has made for a toxic culture."

"Diagnosis?" Kyle leaned forward, curious to hear Sara's insights.

With a compassionate smile, she looked back at Kyle.

"Everyone deserves a second chance. Even Allen Bauerman." The words evoked a return smile and nod of affirmation from Kyle. In a more serious tone Sara continued, "Allen needs to decide if he is willing to take the necessary steps to repair what has been done."

Kyle nodded in agreement. "And what are the necessary steps?"

Sara continued to write in her journal, speaking out loud with the cadence of her pen. "First, recognize the story being told about you as real. Second, identify the story you desire to be told about you beyond the resume–in other words, the authentic you."

"Excellent. Then what?"

Sara continued to write. "Next, create a transformational learning plan toward authentic influence. Step one, define meaningful moments required to change the desired story. This is the authentic you." Sara made a note in the margin of her journal, "This will require new skills."

"What is step two?" Kyle asked.

"Step two. Demonstrate authentic compassion for others."

Kyle let out a slight chuckle after hearing these words, prompting Sara to look up. The look on Sara's face was all Kyle needed to fill in the blanks of his smirk.

"Easier said than done if someone doesn't like people in general," Kyle said, his voice matter of fact. Sara stopped writing to take in Kyle's words. "Compassion for others doesn't come naturally for most. And, I've never been a fan of the 'Fake it until you make it' philosophy. People tend to see through what is inauthentic in the moment," Kyle explained.

"So, what do you do in these cases?" Sara asked.

"People can learn to demonstrate compassion and even, over time, become compassionate. History teaches us it often requires a life-altering moment to bring people to a place where they realize they are powerless to reach on their own. For many, they don't have a reference point for compassion or empathy to work from. It's difficult to show compassion if you've never been shown compassion," Kyle continued as Sara made notes in her journal. "It is possible to put people on the path, but ultimately, they need to shift the focus away from themselves and toward others," Kyle finished. Sara paused, an obvious thought brewing in her mind.

As Sara made notes, she paused and pondered Kyle's words. "Sincere gratitude!" She blurted out. Kyle's expression conveyed promise at the revelation as he nodded for Sara to continue. "Sincere gratitude is a simple technique to focus on what we are currently most grateful for," she said with a bit of excitement in her voice. Beginning to write once again, she said, "When people practice sincere gratitude, they are recording daily what they are most grateful for, which shifts the focus from self to others. Over time, sincere gratitude can lead to increased generosity, even courageous generosity."

"Excellent," Kyle beamed. "Is there a step three?" Sara stared at the page and then scratched out something without saying a word. She looked up to read what she wrote.

"Step three. Be clear and consistent in both word and deed," her voice registered with growing authority.

Kyle nodded enthusiastically. "That sounds like a well thought out framework to move clients toward more authentic influence as a leader," Kyle coached. "Should Allen decide to move in that direction, you will be ready."

Sara gently nodded her head in agreement.

"Just one question," Kyle asked. "Should he decide to do this-and only time will tell if he has the courage it will re-quire-how do you ensure he stays on track? You can't always be with him," Kyle added, already certain of the answer but curious to see how Sara processed the next step. Sara wrote four words in her journal.

"Personal board of directors," she said with confidence.

Kyle leaned back, took the last sip of what was now a chilled cup of coffee, and surveyed a woman who was destined to make an indelible impact on the world.

"My work here is done." Kyle rose to his feet and helped Sara stand to join him. Kyle gave her a gentle hug. "Well done, Sara."

"Thank you, Kyle-for everything." Sara's shoulders relaxed under his support.

Kyle gave her one last squeeze and disappeared out the door, sliding into his waiting car as Mac shut the door.

Sara gathered her journal, placed it in her bag and headed out towards her office in Uptown. As she walked along McK-inney Avenue, her phone began to ring. Looking at the screen, she recognized a FaceTime request from Patterson. Tapping on the screen, the face of Patterson, perched behind Joe's Bar, appeared.

"Hey, Patterson. Everything okay?" Sara asked.

"Yes, ma'am. Just wanted to say hello," Patterson replied with a hint of hesitation. Sara picked up on the delay and jumped right in.

"I'm glad you called. There is something I've been meaning to share with you," Sara began. Patterson stood up a bit straighter as Sara continued to encourage the image on her phone. "As a board member, when we catch up from time to time, we should always ask each other about our high/low for the week." Sara noticed the perplexed look on Patterson's face. "This is really simple, but very powerful. Essentially, we are asking each other to identify the high and low elements of the week and also, what we have learned from it." Patterson began to nod slowly as she understood the concept. "So, let me practice. What has been *your* high and low this week?" Sara challenged.

Taking her time, Patterson slowly responded. "I received the framed picture you sent me from the event this week. Thank you," Patterson added with increased confidence.

"My pleasure, Patterson. And your low?"

"Simon showed up at the bar this week," Patterson revealed, and suddenly, Sara recognized the real reason for the call. Sara stopped dead in her tracks, short of her destination.

"What did he want?"

Patterson paused before answering as she gathered her thoughts. "He was looking for redemption, ma'am," Patterson reported in a resolute tone. "What do you think I should do about that, Sara?" Patterson's face softened, exposing a rare, vulnerable side of herself while her eyes burned through the screen. Sara smiled as she pulled her phone closer.

"Everyone deserves a second chance, blue-eyed Bethany-even Simon Sanders." Sara's voice was reassuring.

"I'm not sure I can do that," Patterson's voice trailed off. "There is more to the story I need to share."

Sara paused then asked, "Would this have anything to do with the press conference Simon has called for later this week?"

Patterson nodded the softly said, "Most likely. I can't be sure."

Sara began putting together some quick details in her mind. "Could this have anything to do with your last mission?" Sara asked.

"Yes, ma'am." Patterson replied. "I'm just worried I will not be up to the challenge. What if it's too much for me to handle? What if I fail?"

Sara appreciated the vulnerability and courage being displayed by Patterson. "That's why I will be there with you. Two are better than one, my friend. The rest of the board will be in the arena with you, too-daring greatly together-because that is what friends do. Failure is rarely fatal in an arena of friends."

With a wink that looked suspiciously similar to Clara Becker, Sara shut off her screen. The noise of the city disappeared as Sara stood quietly at the intersection, the warmth of the new normal washing over her. She gazed at the ring on her finger and the notebook in her hand, symbols of the epic journey ahead of her. Sara smiled warmly as she recalled Clara's final words, *"The best is yet to come."*

"This is the only time I am going to disagree with you, my friend," Sara whispered. "The best is already here."

Sincere
GRATITUDE

Traditionally, in the final pages of most books, mine included, is the often-overlooked page titled, "Acknowledgments." Maybe it's the early morning air or the perfectly brewed fresh coffee, but I am feeling the need to break with tradition.

In the story of *The Changemaker* I came face-to-face with the concepts of sincere gratitude and courageous generosity. Being grateful, I have discovered, is a concept which doesn't come as natural as I wished it would. If you know me well, you've heard me say my writing is more a reminder for myself than a public proclamation to others.

So, for the next several lines of text I want to publicly express my sincere gratitude for the people around me who help me realize my fullest potential. As with any writing project of mine the editor is critical. Mindi Bach worked her magic on *The Newsmaker* and once again brought her A-game to *The Changemaker*. Mindi has the patience of Job to work with someone as challenged as myself, yet her true talent is extracting the very best story possible from each and every character. When it comes to words, she is a true pinball wizard. I am very grateful for Mindi.

The real work of producing a book begins once the story is complete. It is at this point that Stephanie Kemp picks up the pieces and finishes the mosaic. From her winter headquarters at the base of the tallest snowcapped mountains, she displays her unique talent to bring a project of this magnitude to life between snowboarding runs. It must be the fresh air at 15,000 feet that clears her head to see the bigger picture. Her talents are remarkable, and I am truly grateful.

Getting the foreword right is always a challenge. Having one of the top leaders on the planet agree to write the foreword is a true blessing. Lorraine Martin has inspired me from the first day we met. Her consistent character, anchored by her courageous generosity, is the perfect example of authentic influence. I am overwhelmed with gratitude to have her words setting up the story.

The number of people who have endured countless hours of ideas bouncing off whiteboards and text messages is too numerous to record. I am so very grateful for a world class team who encourages me and challenges me daily. Josh Lipscomp, Maria Mercer, Lisa Estes, Carol Jenkins, Tariq Bacchus, Bill Potrykus, Enit Kurian, and Natalie Rea are simply the best.

There are a few, however, who suffered through early, unedited drafts to help me get the story just right. I am deeply grateful for Mia Mends, Daniel Morris, Gail Ciccione, Shelly Slater, Kate Terrell, Laura Schilling, and Marty Martinez for their invaluable insights.

There were several leaders who were my muse for the model of gratitude and generosity. One, who I consider a true inspiration, is Wendy Davidson. In our short time as friends, I have learned what it looks like to lead with authentic influence. I am grateful for her character, which is an example that teaches in both word and deed.

Another person who I am forever grateful for is Kelli Valade, who over the last couple of years has experienced and demonstrated levels of courage and gratitude for life that continue to inspire multitudes of others.

Additionally, the leaders I follow every day inspire me to continue to grow. I am profoundly grateful for Brint Ryan and Ginny Kissling. Their leadership encourages me to pursue excellence in every aspect of life. My desire is to extend that same drive to everyone I come in contact with along the journey.

At the risk of burying the lead, I am most grateful for my family. The blessings surrounding our family would fill another book. What I can say is through the highs and lows of life, my family has taught me the true meaning of sincere gratitude and courageous generosity.

In a world set on a resolute course of continuous change, it is my ever-growing faith in The Lord that grounds me in my enduring love for my family. I realize now, more than ever, it is possible to influence change for the good and not just for change's sake. As a broken person living in a broken world, I am intensely grateful for Hope, which–through it all–guarantees that the best is yet to come.

Tony Bridwell

As an author, international speaker, consultant and coach, Tony Bridwell has been making a difference at some of the world's largest organizations for the past 25 years. He is the author of *The Maker* series, former Chief People Officer of Brinker International and Senior Partner with Partners in Leadership, an international consulting firm. Currently, Tony is the Chief People Officer for the global tax consulting firm, Ryan LLC.

Tony is a highly recognized thought leader in corporate culture, leadership development, and human resources, being named 2015 HR Executive of the Year by DallasHR (the local SHRM affiliate) and also receiving the 2015 Strategic Leadership Award from Strategic Excellence HR.

Tony has been a facilitator and featured speaker for audiences of several thousand people and has presented for multiple conferences and associations, including the CHRO Exchange, DallasHR (SHRM), the HRSouthwest Conference, ATD San Diego, and the California Restaurant Association. Tony is also a member of SHRM and serves on the board of directors for Southwest Transplant Alliance and Taylor's Gift Foundation.

When he is not spending time with his family, Tony turns his efforts toward mentoring a small group of young men, cycling, and writing. With three grown children and three dogs, Tony and his wife, Dee, have called the Dallas area home for almost 30 years.

Visit

TonyBridwell.com

More from Tony Bridwell

The Kingmaker

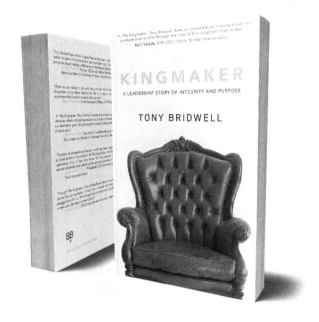

More from Tony Bridwell
The Newsmaker

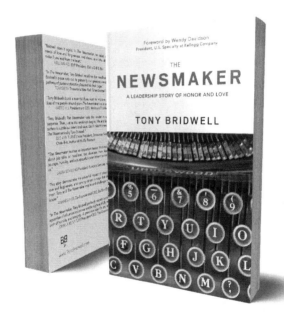

More from Tony Bridwell
The Difference Maker

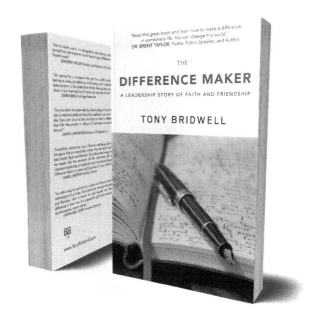